SAINT MARK'S LIFE OF JESUS

SAINT MARK'S LIFE
OF JESUS

TEXTS OF THE LEADERSHIP TRAINING SERIES

1. STANDARD TRAINING SERIES.—A series of studies in the religious needs and capacities of persons of all ages and in ways of dealing with those needs and capacities by means of an effective program of religious education.

2. THE LIVING BOOK SERIES.—A new series of Bible study texts. These texts are of a content nature and are planned to cover the whole Bible.

3. MISSIONS AND SOCIAL STUDIES SERIES.—The texts of this series deal with the interpretation and practical application of the Christian religion.

4. COKESBURY SERIES.—A series of texts designed specifically to meet the needs of the small school by enabling workers to come to a clearer understanding and a more adequate appreciation of their problems and to acquire greater skill in handling them.

SAINT MARK'S LIFE OF JESUS

BY

ANDREW SLEDD, Ph.D. (Yale)

PROFESSOR OF GREEK AND NEW TESTAMENT LITERATURE
EMORY UNIVERSITY

THE LIVING BOOK SERIES
E. B. CHAPPELL, EDITOR

NASHVILLE, TENN.
COKESBURY PRESS
1930

LEADERSHIP TRAINING SERIES

BIBLE COURSE

FOREWORD

THE "Bible Course" will consist of a series of Bible texts or units of twelve chapters each. Each volume is to deal with a single book of the Bible, or with some important aspect of Bible study, except that in case of the shorter books of the Bible two or more books will sometimes be treated in a single volume. Ultimately it is proposed to extend this series of brief Bible texts to cover practically the entire Bible.

The arrangement of these studies in comparatively brief volumes is designed to encourage Sunday school and other Christian workers to take up this course volume by volume as they have opportunity, so that in time they may make an intelligent, careful study of the entire Bible. The books of this course are to be used as a basis of Bible study, being so written as to encourage the study of the Bible text itself.

The Bible Course follows as a logical sequel to the Standard Training Course. That course, while providing a certain amount of Bible study, is primarily devoted to a study of the pupil, his nature and needs, and the laws of learning—that is, to the principles and processes of religious education—and is designed to give illumination and guidance to teachers of religion in their approach to their task. It was never assumed that the brief amount of Bible study that it has been possible to embrace in the

Standard Training Course provided more than a mere beginning in Bible study.

In projecting a course of training for teachers of religion it was necessary to begin with the study of the nature and needs of the pupil and the principles and processes of religious education. But the process can have significance only with reference to the end in view. The objective must be the enthronement of Jesus Christ in every life and the fulfillment of every life in a Christlike character and in Christian service.

The time has come when, in addition to training offered in child nature, pedagogy, and methods of Sunday school work, more attention must be given to content and background in the furnishing of our Sunday school workers.

The task in training teachers and leaders for the work of religious education is to help them to understand Christ and his message in relation to their own lives and the lives of their pupils and in relation to the pressing problems of our own world with all its complex and tragic needs.

It is necessary to continue a program of training in principles and processes. At the same time larger attention must be given to the interpretation of the religion of Christ in its essential and dynamic bearing upon all the issues of life.

In line with this view of training, the Bible Course and also the Missions and Social Service Course are now being prepared, which, together with the Standard Training Course already in use, constitute the Leadership Training Series. These three courses are all on the same general level of thoroughness.

6

CONTENTS

CHAPTER I

CHAPTER II

CHAPTER III

CHAPTER IV

CHAPTER V

CHAPTER VI

CHAPTER VII

CHAPTER VIII

CHAPTER IX

CHAPTER X

CHAPTER XI

CHAPTER XII

INTRODUCTION

THE Gospel of Mark is our earliest Life of Jesus, and provides the narrative framework for all subsequent Lives of the same type. Hence its choice as the basis of this book.

Mark was not a personal follower of Jesus in his lifetime; but, as a youth, he was in touch with the primitive Christian community in Jerusalem, which met in his mother's house, and he may very well have seen the Master. As a young man, he was the friend and associate both of Peter and of Paul, being the companion of Paul and Barnabas on their first missionary journey and the interpreter of Peter in his preaching. Some years later, when Peter and Paul were prisoners in Rome, Mark is again with them and is spoken of by each of them in terms of affectionate esteem.

From his service to Peter as his interpeter Mark derived some, at least, of the material for his gospel; and it would be surprising if his contacts with Paul had not influenced him in his understanding and interpretation of that material. But his gospel is not a fragmentary collection of Petrine Memorabilia. Its material, as a whole, is organized with great skill. The organizing principle has a strong Pauline color, and the resultant work gives us the most compact and the clearest outline of the life, as distinguished from the teaching, of Jesus that has come down to us.

The purpose of this book is to put the uncritical reader into possession of this outline as a background for his further studies. It is in no sense another or a new "Life of Jesus." It is an attempt which, without mock modesty, can be characterized as only partially successful, to reproduce the course and stages of Jesus' ministry as they appear in our oldest Gospel, with only such deepening of lines as may be needed to make the ancient picture stand out more clearly. It would be rash to suppose that we can see Jesus through the eyes of the first century, but doubtless we may come nearer to that than we commonly do; and it is hoped that this book may justify its existence in that direction by helping to make him a somewhat more substantial and definite historical figure.

The most comprehensive acknowledgment should be made of indebtedness to others. The writer has been long interested in the Gospel of Mark, and that interest has drawn in material, suggestive and substantial, from divers sources. Direct quotations are, of course, duly indicated; but suggestions have often been assimilated and their source forgotten; often, too, they have been taken over and recast in accordance with the writer's own ideas and to suit the purposes of his work. In such cases, definite acknowledgment of obligation has seemed impracticable, if not impossible; but it should be said that Professor Bacon's "Beginnings of Gospel Story" and Professor Menzies' "The Earliest Gospel" have been particularly helpful in this way, and are due the special and grateful acknowledgment which is here given them.

And may all that has been said be for the greater glory of God and of his Son, Jesus Christ, our Lord!

ANDREW SLEDD.

EMORY UNIVERSITY, GA.,
September 10, 1926.

CHAPTER I

THE BACKGROUND AND ENVIRONMENT OF JESUS

THE Gospel of Mark has nothing to say of the birth and early life of Jesus. It introduces him, already grown, at the time of his baptism by John, and records only incidents from the brief but crowded period of his public ministry. In the course of this record, however, certain conditions are assumed, certain allusions made, and certain facts incidentally appear that throw some light upon the earlier period and need to be borne in mind for the understanding of his adult career.

1. THE HOME

(a) Jesus' home at the time of his baptism was at Nazareth in Galilee (1: 9).

Family and Station (b) His mother's name was Mary, and he had four brothers—James and Joses, and Judas and Simon—and at least two sisters (6: 3).

(c) He was a carpenter by trade, and was not regarded as one of the learned or leading men of his home community (6: 2, 3).

(d) The status of his associates and most intimate friends confirms the implication of his own trade that he belonged to the working classes, the great lower middle class of society. "A vital element in Jesus' power over the masses lay in his belonging to the wage-earning class" (Bacon, Mark 6: 3).

(e) The only other mention of the family of Jesus in Mark is found in 3: 21 and 31–35. There they sought to

11

restrain him in his intense activity; "for they said, He is beside himself"; and Jesus, "looking round on them which sat about him, saith, Behold my mother and my brethren." And in Nazareth later he said, "A prophet is not without honor, save in his own country, and among his own kin, and in his own house" (6: 4).

2. THE SCHOOL

The Gospel has nothing to say of the schooling of Jesus. We know, however, of the emphasis laid in the Old Testament upon the religious instruction of the young; and it is said that from about 75 B.C., it was required by law of all Jewish boys that they should attend the synagogue school from their sixth to their twelfth year. The matter of instruction both in the home and in the synagogue school was exclusively religious and the textbook was exclusively the Old Testament. Whence we may fairly conclude that Jesus received the usual religious instruction in the home and in the synagogue school, despite the silence of the Gospels on this point. And the Gospels themselves show clearly that in his manhood Jesus possessed an extensive knowledge of the Scriptures, traditions, and institutions of his people— the beginnings of which are to be found, doubtless, in his youthful training; but the insight into, and grasp of, these matters, the evaluation and interpretation, were not only not of the school, but were beyond and contrary to its instruction.

Jesus was schooled indeed; but he was not of the schools. His title to be called Rabbi was intrinsic and not conventional. His world was his schoolhouse, and the response of his own profound and sensitive spirit to the facts that it

Usual Instruction

brought him, from past and present, from God and man and nature, constituted his education. We cannot put our hands upon his master; we cannot classify him in any "school." He was a child in his Father's house, a genius, a prophet—yea, and I say unto you, much more than a prophet.

But the Jewish world of Jesus' day (in Palestine, especially) was school-ridden. The stolid complacency of its erudition and its piety had no place for an original and creative spirit. Its rabbis, with their pseudo-erudition, sat in the seats of the mighty; and the schoolman, with his proud but puerile scholasticism, was the critic and opponent of the carpenter-prophet of Nazareth. His new wine could not be poured into the old skins of their established system.

3. THE NATION

Inheritance and Environment

Inheritance and environment both influence developing personality and condition its expression. In a very large sense, every man is the child of his age; and his age is the child of its predecessors. There is, indeed, a fullness of time, when the currents of the past, in the history of institutions and of the human spirit, converge upon a change and enter a new channel; but the new stream cannot be cut off from its sources nor understood apart from them. Jesus was born in such a fullness of time. He grew to manhood when and where great streams converged. His personality was colored by his time and place; and his self-expression was conditioned by them. This was, indeed, a part of the fullness of time itself. Though his spirit was timeless and placeless, it was embodied in time

13

and place; and the Jesus of history cannot be understood or interpreted apart from his land and age.

(a) *Political*. As a matter of fact, Jesus' world was under Roman sway; as a matter of popular sentiment, it was cherishing memories and entertaining hopes not at all consonant with that supremacy.

The Jews had been permitted to return from the Exile, and, after a century of struggle and disappointment, had finally established a religious state under Persian control, about 450 B.C. A hundred years later Persian power had been broken by Alexander of Macedon, and Palestine, and the rest of the East, passed under Macedonian supremacy. After the death of Alexander, Palestine was a bone of contention between Egypt and Syria, but finally fell under the control of Syria about 200 B.C.

Alexander had conceived the idea of unifying his vast dominions by the spread among them of a common culture, Hellenization which was, naturally, that of the conqueror. Greek language, life, and religion were to reduce to a common base the distinguishing and generally antagonistic characteristics of the peoples of his empire. When Palestine finally fell into the hands of Syria, Antiochus IV, called by his friends Epiphanes, "The Manifest (God)," and by his enemies Epimanes, "The Madman," who seized the throne in 175 B.C., sought to apply this principle systematically to the Jews. But not content with peaceful penetration, under which the process was making considerable progress, especially among the "moderns" and the younger generation, and finding certain elements unreasonably recalcitrant, especially in regard to the religion of their fathers, Antiochus undertook to bring the process to consummation by the use of force. As

14

stubborn adherence to the Jewish faith was the main obstacle in his way, he directed the force of his attack against that point. He plundered and polluted the Temple, even going so far as to offer, in 168 B.C., the sacrifice of a sow to Zeus upon the altar of burnt offering. He forbade the reading or the possession of the books of the Law, the circumcision of the children, and the other characteristic and precious rites and privileges of the Jewish faith, and ordered the people instead to offer sacrifices to pagan gods throughout the land. And these prohibitions and commands were enforced with the utmost severity, so that even mothers who ventured to have their children circumcised were slain with their dead babies about their necks.

But in his violence Antiochus overreached himself and defeated his own plans. The inevitable reaction took place, and the Jews revolted. The revolt was **Maccabean Revolt** precipitated by the action of an old man of priestly family, Mattathias by name, a resident of the little village of Modin, some twelve miles northwest of Jerusalem. When the officer of the king assembled the villagers to take part in a heathen sacrifice, Mattathias not only refused to participate but slew both the officer and a renegade Jew who was about to take part in the offering. He then took to the hills and, gathering about him a little band of patriots, began an apparently hopeless struggle against Syria, the main motive and energy of which was the preservation of the religion of his people against the assaults of paganism.

Mattathias had five sons, who cast in their lot with their father and carried on his work after his death. Judas, "the hammerer" ("Maccabee," whence the family name, "The

15

Maccabees"), was the greatest general, and was so successful in his campaigns that just three years after the defilement of the temple by Antiochus it was cleansed and, in a sense, rededicated to the service of Jehovah; whence the Feast of Dedication, celebrated with great enthusiasm and joy in the days of our Lord. Simon, another son, was the greatest diplomat; and after the death of his more warlike brother, Judas, in 161 B.C., and the capture of Jonathan in 143 B.C., Simon so manipulated the political situation as to win the political independence of Judea, about 142 B.C. Under Simon and his successors the borders of the new state were extended both east and north until it rivaled in area the ancient kingdom of David.

For eighty years the new state continued—a sovereign Jewish state, enjoying political as well as religious independence. But in 63 B.C. the Romans laid their **Liberty Lost** hands upon it, reducing it anew to a condition of vassalage, from which it was never freed .Religious liberty and a certain measure of local autonomy were left; but political independence was lost, and any movements that contemplated or implied its reassertion were jealously watched and rigorously repressed by the representatives of sovereign Rome.

Jesus was born within sixty years of this subjugation of his people. At his birth, and long thereafter, there were many old people who remembered that sad day, and many families that cherished the memory of the heroic part that ancestors but lately dead had played in the Maccabean struggle for the law and the state and of the days of independence they had won; for Jesus' birthday was only thirty years farther from the beginning of the Maccabean struggle than we are from the beginning of our Revolutionary War. Indeed, if we may suppose (for the sake of illustration) that each of Jesus' ancestors in the Lukan genealogy was fifty years old when the succeeding son was born, Joseph's great-grandfather, Levi, was a man between thirty and forty years of age when the Maccabean struggle began, and Joseph's father, Heli, was about forty years old when the political independence of the nation was lost to Rome. Levi may have played a part in the struggle at its beginning, and Heli at its close, so close was it to the days of Jesus.

But no high-spirited people will so easily lose their independence, forget the privileges of that state, or despair

Hopes

of its restoration. We have ample evidence that the Jews were neither forgetful nor despairing. They looked and longed for their new deliverer. Simeon (whose name was the same as that of the great-grandfather of Judas Maccabeus), in the temple, was ready to depart in peace, "for mine eyes have seen thy salvation, which thou hast prepared before the face of all peoples"; and the aged Anna, who had been a mature woman when independence was lost, spake of the infant Jesus "to all them that were looking for the redemption of Jerusalem" (Luke 2: 30, 38). The people's Messianic hopes had been disappointed in Zerubbabel, and in the Maccabees, but they had not been destroyed. And Jesus was born in an atmosphere still redolent of the recent struggle, and quivering with the expectation of a deliverer who should "restore the kingdom unto Israel" (Acts 1: 6). He grew up in this atmosphere: and the recognition of this fact and its influence is imperative for any understanding of his life

Discontent

and work. In a word, Jesus was the child of a people who had fallen recently under Roman

2   17

sway, many of whom were profoundly discontented with that condition and eager for deliverance therefrom. His inheritance, therefore, was one of a love of liberty and recent, though brief, enjoyment of it. His political environment, outwardly, was that of domination by a foreign and pagan power; but beneath the surface there was widespread repudiation of that domination, and, in some classes, readiness to throw it off by force of arms, while in others there was an eager expectation of divine deliverance by supernatural means.

(b) *Cultural.* While the efforts for the complete Hellenization of the Jews had been brought to naught by the Maccabean struggle, Greek life and culture were not without a widespread influence. There were many Greek towns in Galilee, and the Decapolis was originally a league of ten Greek cities, with their adjacent territory, and in these towns the life and worship and speech were predominantly Greek. The Greek language, indeed, not in its classic form, but in a colloquial form known as the *Koinê*, was both the official language of the Roman Empire for the eastern provinces and the most common medium of communication in all parts of the Mediterranean world. The Old Testament Scriptures had been translated into Greek; and, though Jesus himself probably used the ancient Hebrew Old Testament, the New Testament writers used almost entirely the Greek version. Other religious literature not included in our Old Testament was current in Greek, either written in that tongue or translated into it, and with some of this it seems almost certain that Jesus was familiar.

Greek Culture

But Greek influence in the world of Jesus was not limited to a widespread language. Greek elegance of life, Greek

18

fondness for, and Greek forms of, amusement had also penetrated Palestine and greatly influenced considerable classes of the Jewish people. Greek philosophy also and Greek religion were neither unknown nor without their devotees both Greek and Jewish.

The inscription upon the cross, which John (19: 20) says "was written in Hebrew, and in Latin, and in Greek," will give some idea of the cosmopolitan nature of the world into which Jesus came. All these influences entered in varying degrees into the people to whom Jesus ministered, the audiences to which he spoke, and therefore conditioned the interpretation of his life and message. But Jesus' own associates and associations were chiefly Jewish. And these alien elements, which so largely affected his gospel in its transmission and interpretation, had apparently little effect upon himself. That they contributed to his breadth of view and sympathy, thus playing their part
Jesus a
Jew in making him the world figure that he became, need not be denied; but, at the same time, it must be maintained that he was, first and last, a Jew of his age and people. And the elements that separated him from them were not alien, but rather the ancient and peculiar glories of his people.

(c) *Religious*. The foregoing is especially true in the religious area. Whatever alien elements, especially Greek, the religion of Jesus may have taken on in its Pauline (and other) interpretations, for Jesus himself it was the ancient prophetic (and more recent apocalyptic) message of his people, deepened and enriched indeed, "fulfilled," but not fulfilled by the introduction of alien innovations, but by the resuscitation and extension of the ancient lines of faith and hope.

19

With the Exile popular idolatry had ceased. Never thereafter did the people as a whole turn aside to follow strange gods. They had at last become, in a peculiar and definite sense, the people of Jehovah; and this fact lies at the basis of their subsequent history and explains why there are no denunciations of Jewish idolatry in the New Testament. Nevertheless, the Exile had radically modified the older ideas of ritual and worship, and the influence of this modification survived the return and the reëstablishment of the Jewish Church-State. With the people scattered, the temple in ruins, and its ritual, primarily sacrificial, no longer possible, the religion of Jehovah, if it was to survive at all, must perforce become communal and individual rather than national, with a corresponding depression of its formal and exaltation of its inner aspects and requirements. Jeremiah is said to have "discovered the individual," and his predecessors had long before proclaimed that the religion of Jehovah is righteousness rather than ritual; and these great lessons, enforced by the experiences of the Exile, were never wholly lost among the people. Despite the retrogression of post-exilic times, many simple Jews could repeat with reverence and understanding the words of their psalmist, "Sacrifice and burnt offering thou wouldest not, else would I bring it; a humble and a contrite heart, O Lord, thou wilt not refuse." (Ps. 51: 17.)

Individual Piety

The synagogue seems to have been the outgrowth of this situation. This "characteristic institution of Judaism," which meets us on nearly every page of the New Testament, is named only once in the Old Testament. (But compare the meetings of the elders in the house of Ezekiel, mentioned in Ezekiel 8: 1 and 20: 1.)

Synagogue

20

In Psalm 74: 8 we read: "They have burned up all the synagogues of God in the land"—which implies that the synagogues were numerous when the Psalmist wrote, while other statements in the Psalm indicate their importance in the national and religious life. Now this Psalm was probably written about 350 B.C., so that sometime before this date synagogues had already become important and widespread institutions.

The great reform under Ezra and Nehemiah (457-444 B.C.), if it did not originate, certainly demanded for its success an institution like the synagogue. These leaders proposed to organize the whole life of the people around "the Law of Moses." To this end they read and interpreted the Law in public assembly (444 B.C.); and the people thereupon bound themselves by an oath to accept and observe it (Nehemiah, chapters 8-10). They thus adopted a written code, which of itself, aside from the specific covenants and provisions, tended to separate them from other nations and make them a peculiar people; and they became the people of a book, and created the first canon of the Old Testament Scriptures. A generation before the fall of Jerusalem similar action had been taken by the people with reference to the book of Deuteronomy under good King Josiah (621 B.C.). Whether the course of Ezra and Nehemiah was influenced by this precedent, they went much further, and the effects of their reform were more profound and lasting.

The Law

But if a people is to keep a fixed body of laws, they must be instructed therein; and the laws themselves must be interpreted. The course of Ezra and Nehemiah at the adoption of the code must be continually repeated with the birth of new generations and the

Scribes

21

expansion of the people. Hence a need for instructors and interpreters, and for places and times for their work, all tending of themselves to emphasize the separateness of those who had the Law from those who had it not. Hence, also, the development of a growing body of interpretations around the central Law, which would tend, with age and repetition, to acquire equality with the Law itself, and might even overshadow and pervert the Law.

Between the days of Ezra and the Maccabean struggle the situation just described unfolded in its natural and logical development; and, accentuated, and in particulars modified, by the causes which precipitated the Maccabean revolt and by the issue thereof, gave rise to many of the most important elements in the religious inheritance and environment of Jesus. Thus:

(1) The separateness of the people from their pagan neighbors, enforced in the reform of Ezra and Nehemiah, left also a deep and abiding hostility between

Separation

the Jews and their neighbors the Samaritans. The latter took over the Pentateuch, in their own form (the Samaritan Pentateuch), but did not receive any of the later canonized Scriptures of the Jews, nor the body of traditions which gathered around them. About 400 B.C., they built their own temple to Jehovah on Mount Gerizim, and, though this temple was destroyed along with their capital city Samaria when they were brought under Jewish supremacy in the Maccabean days (by John Hyrcanus), the site was still held sacred and the Samaritans worshiped Jehovah there in the days of Jesus, as the handful of their descendants does even to this day.

With the rest of the Maccabean kingdom, Samaria fell under the control of Rome in B.C. 63 and was governed

22

by Herod the Great at the time of Jesus' birth. When
Herod died, Samaria, along with Judea, fell to his son
Archelaus; and when Archelaus was banished both districts
were attached to the province of Syria and governed by
Roman procurators resident at Cæsarea in Judea. This
was the political situation at the time of Jesus' death.
But such political relationship could not bring Jews and
Samaritans together; and in the days of Jesus not only did
"Jews have no dealings with Samaritans" (John 4: 9b),
but their attitude, reciprocated by the Samaritans, was
one of profound hostility and contempt.

(2) Moreover, this separateness of the Jews was peculiarly and insidiously threatened by the spread of Hellenism
after the death of Alexander the Great. As
has been said above, not all the Jews were opposed to this movement; and from this difference of attitude
arose deep and lasting differences among the leaders of the
people. The party that sympathized with the spread of this
culture, to which the priests and the wealthy aristocracy in
the main belonged, was sharply differentiated from the party
of protest and opposition, which was composed of those more
loyal to their inherited institutions, with their followers
among the common people. By the time of the Maccabean
struggle the latter group had come to be known as the Hasi-
deans (Chasidim, in Hebrew), or "The Pious," and it evolved
into the Pharisees and Essenes of the days of Jesus; while
the priestly aristocratic group was known as the Sadducees,
deriving its party name probably from the Zadoc who
succeeded Abiathar in the priesthood in the days of Solo-
mon (1 Kings 1: 7, 8; 2: 26–35), and from whose descendants "the high priests were taken till the time of the Maccabees" (compare Ezekiel 40: 46; 44: 15).

Sects

23

The Pharisees were thus, from the first, a religious sect.
In the Maccabean struggle, the Pious lost interest with the
achievement of religious liberty, and were either
Pharisees indifferent or antagonistic to the prosecution of the
struggle for political independence. They continued to
stand aloof from politics, except where their religious interests were directly involved, leaving, as they claimed, the political destiny of the nation in the hands of God, which meant,
in effect, in the hands of the politicians. They held that the
good Jew's part for the realization of the national hope lay in
making ready for the divine interposition—that God would
redeem Israel when Israel should be ripe for redemption,
and that Israel would be ready when all the Law should be
observed by all the people. Hence an ever-increasing
emphasis upon the Law, its minute interpretation, its careful and scrupulous observance, and its accurate imparta-
tion not only to the Jews, but to such Gentiles as would
receive it. (For Jesus' drastic criticism of their missionary
activity and its results, see Matthew 23: 15.) Hence, also,
the apocalyptic form of the Messianic hope, as it appears
in Pharisaic (and early Christian) literature down to the
close of the first century A.D. (See below.)

Now it cannot be denied that there was much good in the
Pharisees in the earlier stages of the history and activities
of the sect. They protected the precious de-
Their Services posit of the Jewish faith when their world was
thrown into the Grecian melting pot. Their
very separateness insured the preservation of a peculiar
people. They emphasized the sovereignty and sufficiency
of God, the one, only God; and they looked to him for
national deliverance in his own good time. By their aloof-
ness from politics they established and maintained the

24

separation of Church and State, so that the former might survive though the latter perished. They devoted themselves to teaching; and their very emphasis upon the Law maintained a relatively high standard of faith and practice among the people. It is therefore no wonder that the sect, though actually small in numbers in the days of Jesus—there are said to have been only 6,000—attained an unrivaled position of religious influence and leadership. They presented to the common people the inherited religion of the law in its purest and strictest form, including, without discrimination, many actually later acquisitions, such as the resurrection, and the apocalyptic hope, which had now become themselves traditional.

The Pharisees of the Gospels represent the extremes of these tendencies, original good that by perverted emphasis has become the enemy of the better and the best. Their separateness has become a haughty, vain, and intolerant class consciousness. Their God has become *their* God. And their emphasis upon the Law and its interpretations has enslaved them to the letter and the traditions of the elders, so that they have become fossilized formalists, without a sense of need or an idea that other than apocalyptic change might be desirable, without even an apprehension of the vast and eternally creative dynamic of a spiritual life. Between them and Jesus, or indeed any prophetic spirit, like that of John the Baptist, there was an irrepressible conflict. The old skins, dry and hardened, could not hold the new wine of the gospel.

Defects

The Sadducees, as has been said, were the priestly-aristocratic party. Their main interests were political, and their main attitude conservative. Religiously, they were ritualistic and reactionary; politically,

Sadducees

25

they were standpatters and opportunists. They emphasized the written law, as ritual, however, not as righteousness; and in this emphasis upon the code, they rejected the oral law, and the doctrinal novelties, such as the resurrection, which the Pharisees had taken up and transmitted to the people. Socially and politically, as well as religiously, they were concerned with maintaining the *status quo*, or, if a new status were inevitable, with maintaining their position therein. Naturally, therefore, they had little or no part in the Messianic hope, and were very definitely opposed to any Messianic agitation.

These facts, especially the last stated, will explain the attitude of the Sadducees toward Jesus and the early Church. The opposition of the Pharisees was religious: Jesus would undermine the traditions and the Law; that of the Sadducees was political: Jesus would disturb the public peace.

The Pharisees were from first to last the better sect; but, by different roads, both sects had reached a point in the days of Jesus when they could make no place for a prophetic spirit. For a prophet is always a disturber, a menace to things as they are; and all classes of the regulars, of whatever differences among themselves and whatever diversity of motive, are at one in their opposition to him.

(3) *The Hope.* There was, however, in all this situation, one element that contained the impulse and the promise of imminent change, and that was the Messianic hope. Everything that accentuated the separateness of the Jewish people, their literature, institutions, and traditions, contributed to their discontent under the alien domination of Rome, and, in the same measure, to the vitality and vividness of their ancient hope of deliverance. The God

of their fathers had not permanently cast off his people; nor had he lost either the will or the power to deliver them. He would not abandon them, or leave them forever in their low estate of humiliation and subjection. But sometime, somehow, he would, for his own name's sake, raise up for them a deliverer, or himself immediately intervene in their behalf, that their ancient estate of honor and of power might be restored and enlarged among, or over, the nations of the world that knew him not. And the worse their present state, the brighter this hope and the nearer its realization.

This hope had deep and ancient roots in the covenant and promises of God, and received fresh impulse in the Maccabean struggles, and, in the days of Roman supremacy, including the days of Jesus, burned fiercely below the surface and frequently broke through the thin crust of outward acceptance of the existing order, now in lurid apocalyptic vision and now in actual revolt.

Ancient

It was the most vivid and potent factor in the joint political and religious life and hopes of the Jewish people in the days of Jesus.

Vivid

As the roots of this hope were religio-political, so was its end, which was the restoration of the kingdom unto Israel, the reëstablishment of the old theocracy, the final setting up of the kingdom of God. But the processes by which it was conceived that this end should be achieved were of two different forms according as they emphasized human instrumentalities or relied exclusively upon the supernatural, divine intervention for its accomplishment.

The Kingdom

Both parties were looking for a Messiah; but to the one, which was largely of the common people, and especially

27

strong in Galilee, and which found definite organization and expression in the Zealots (compare Simon, the Cananæan, or the Zealot, among the apostles of Jesus, Mark 3: 18), this Messiah would be a military and political leader, especially equipped by God for the work of deliverance with the sword; to the other, which was largely of the Pharisees, this Messiah would be a purely heavenly being, whom God would supernaturally send in his own good time, who would by his supernatural power deliver the chosen people from their oppressors and set up among them, and for them, the kingdom of God.

Militant and Apocalyptic

But the coming of the Messiah was imminent, and with his coming the establishment of the kingdom of God. For two centuries, from the overthrow of the Maccabees by Rome in 63 B.C., to the final destruction of the nation in the revolt of Bar-Cochba in 135 A.D., this hope was quick and eager in the hearts of the Jews of Palestine; and they were prompt to ask of any new figure of prominence whether he might be the Christ, and to follow any leader who laid claim to that office and promised them an early realization of their hopes.

Messiah at Hand

This situation is particularly vivid in the opening chapters of the Gospel of Luke. "And as the people were in expectation, and all men reasoned in their hearts concerning John, whether haply he were the Christ; John answered, saying unto them all, I indeed baptize you with water; but there cometh he that is mightier than I, the latchet of whose shoes I am not worthy to unloose: he shall baptize you with the Holy Spirit and with fire; whose fan is in his hand, thoroughly to cleanse his threshing-floor, and to gather the wheat into his garner; but the chaff he will burn

up with unquenchable fire" (Luke 3: 15–17). This statement both expresses and lays hold upon the Messianic
hopes of the people; and indicates one of the most significant factors in the background and environment of
Jesus.

29

CHAPTER II

THE APPEARANCE OF JESUS AND THE BEGINNING OF HIS WORK

MARK 1: 1–3: 6

INTO such an atmosphere of eager expectation came John the Baptist, in fulfillment of the ancient prophecy, "Behold, I send my messenger before thy face, who shall prepare thy way; the voice of one crying in the wilderness, Make ye ready the way of the Lord, make his paths straight" (Mark 1: 2–4; Isa. 40: 3; Mal. 3: 1). And John's appearance and message were the beginning of the good news about Jesus Christ, for he both centralized the Messianic expectations of the people and focused them upon the One who should come after him.

John the Baptist

John had the appearance, habits, and mode of life of one of the ancient prophets, particularly of Elijah; and his appearance and preaching created widespread and profound excitement. For he preached, and symbolized by his rite of baptism, the Great Repentance that should precede and initiate the Messianic Era, and announced the coming of the Mightier One, who should baptize not with water but with the Holy Spirit. The interest in John's ministry is, therefore, purely Messianic; he came in accordance with the Prophecy; he preached the Great Repentance; and he announced the Coming One.

But John fulfilled certain other elements in the popular Messianic expectation. There was a Jewish belief that "the Christ, if he has indeed been born, and exists anywhere, is unknown, and does not even

Elijah

30

know himself, and has no power, until Elias come to anoint him, and make him manifest to all" (Justin Martyr, Dial. 8). John fulfilled this expectation. "How is it that the scribes say that Elijah must first come?" asked the apostles of Jesus. And he answered, "But I say unto you, that Elijah is come, and they have done unto him whatsoever they would, even as it is written of him" (Mark 9: 11-13).

And so when Jesus came from Nazareth of Galilee, and was baptized by John, this baptism was his Messianic anointing by the Elijah-forerunner, and was accompanied by the descent of the Spirit upon him, equipping him for his Messianic work, as indicated in the voice from heaven, saying, "Thou art my beloved Son, in thee I am well pleased."*

Messianic Anointing of Jesus

Immediately after the baptism the Spirit, who had then entered Jesus, thrust him forth into the wilderness, the haunt of the demons. And there for forty days Jesus was engaged in a mighty conflict with Satan, and successfully withstood all his assaults, thus at once vindicating the testimony to his Sonship given at the baptism, indicating his supremacy over the great enemy of God and man, and presaging the breaking of his power and the overthrow of his dominion. And "he was with the wild beasts (unharmed), and the angels ministered unto him" (Mark 1: 13).

Conflict with Satan

It will thus appear that the controlling purpose of this prologue is to set forth the Messiahship of Jesus; and it is this purpose that leads the Evangelist to reduce the ministry of John and the temptation of Jesus to their simplest Messianic elements.

Purpose of This Prologue

*Compare the calls of Old Testament Prophets, as that of Isaiah, described in Isaiah 6.

31

He would have his readers understand at the beginning that the Jesus whose earthly career he is about to sketch was in truth the Messiah, the Son of God. That is, indeed, his thesis.

How long Jesus remained in Judea after these preliminary incidents, we do not know. But after John was cast into prison (as related in Mark 6: 14–29), Jesus returned to Galilee and there began his own public ministry; and at the forefront of that ministry is set a condensed outline of his message, which was a continuation of the message of John, and affords a key to the narrative of the work and teaching of Jesus that now follows. "Jesus came into Galilee, preaching the gospel of God (the good tidings sent from God), and saying, The time is fulfilled, and the kingdom of God is at hand: repent ye, and be lieve in the gospel (good tidings)" (Mark 1: 14, 15).

Jesus Returns to Galilee

His Message

Jesus thus began his ministry as the announcer of impending change. That change was in accordance with the divine purpose, whose maturing is indicated in the words, "The time is fulfilled." The result of the change will be a new order, described as "the kingdom of God," which, because the time is fulfilled, is now "at hand." This is the good tidings sent from God.

This kingdom of God is not specifically defined. The phrase is not new, and it is assumed that it will be understood.* Qualitatively, indeed — though this does not

*To Jesus' Jewish hearers the words meant a new religio-political order in which the people of God's ancient choice would be liberated from foreign domination and given a position of primacy (under God's Anointed, Christ) among the nations of the earth. As in the words of Zacharias, the father of the Baptist, the appearance of the kingdom meant "salvation from our enemies, and from the hand of

appear in this initial announcement—this kingdom is already present in Jesus and his followers; but
The Kingdom Near factually, objectively, it is yet to come. But this coming is near, at hand; and it will soon take place in apocalyptic fashion through the immediate intervention of God, either directly or in the person of his representative. And, since the kingdom is thus a new order, divinely purposed and to be divinely inaugurated, and since repentance is a condition of participation in it, the nearness of the kingdom necessitates immediate action and gives urgency to the call to repent. Any real belief in the good tidings of the kingdom's coming must lead to repentance as a preparation for it.

The refusal of the people to accept this announcement of Jesus will not affect its truth. For the kingdom is soon coming, because the time appointed by God is
Possible Consequences fulfilled; and the announcement merely gives the people an opportunity either to believe and repent or to refuse to do so. If the nation will receive the message, it will become, with divine favor, the embodiment of the kingdom. But a refusal of the message will be fraught with momentous consequences both for the nation and for Jesus and his followers. For the nation there will be ruin, for nothing may stand in the way of the realization of the divine purpose. For Jesus and his followers there will be temporary suffering, and even death, at the hands

---

all that hate us." Now did God "remember his holy covenant; the oath which he sware to Abraham our father, to grant unto us that we being delivered out of the hand of our enemies should serve him without fear, in holiness and righteousness before him all our days" (Luke 1: 67ff.). And Jesus' first hearers certainly understood his message as a promise of such deliverance and of a "restoration of the kingdom unto Israel" (Acts 1: 6).

of the unbelieving, in the interim between the announcement and the consummation. But at the consummation, and that soon, they will be gloriously vindicated; and the kingdom that is already qualitatively theirs will be theirs factually and objectively, to the humiliation and conviction of all those who have refused to believe.

This negative aspect—refusal, and its consequences—does not appear at the very first. It is only implicit in the first brief announcement of Jesus' message. But it soon comes to the front, as will be seen; and the whole course of Jesus' ministry is determined by the unfolding of its possibilities.

Thus the opening events of his ministry fall into two clearly marked and closely related divisions. It is a period of intense public activity and great popular excitement, in which (1) Jesus wins great popularity with the masses of the people, so that it seems that his message will be received (Mark 1: 14, 45); but (2), partly because of this popularity, and partly because of certain aspects of his message and behavior, he soon encounters increasing criticism and hostility on the part of the leaders of the people, religious and political, and they determine not only to reject his message but to put him to death as the only way to break his influence and check the consequences of his activity (Mark 2: 1-3, 6). And this cleavage in the early reception of Jesus underlies all the following narrative.

Favor and Opposition

(1) Jesus had already determined to enlist the help of others in his enterprise—a step that, even should his message be received by all who heard it, commended itself for many reasons, not the least being the urgency of the situation and the brevity of

Peter and Others Called

34

the time at his disposal. And so, soon after his return to Galilee, as he was walking along the shore of the Sea of Galilee, famous for its fisheries, and saw the fisher brothers, Simon and Andrew, and James and John, engaged in the work of their occupation, he invited them to follow him, and so to change their occupation to that of "fishers of men." Their response may be attributed to the immediate impression of the personality of Jesus, or it may indicate some previous knowledge of him—though Mark gives no intimation of such knowledge; for they immediately abandoned their work and attached themselves to the person of the Master; and thus these four constituted the first, as they later became the innermost, group of his intimates and helpers.

Simon and Andrew lived in Capernaum (Nahum's Village), on the northwestern side of the sea. There they had a house, which now became the headquarters of Jesus for the remainder of his ministry in Galilee. And the first detailed scene in that ministry is the following account of the activities of a single Sabbath in Capernaum (1: 21-38).

Jesus attended the synagogue worship that Sabbath morning, and, already known as a teacher, embraced the opportunity offered to speak to the congregation. (Compare Acts 13: 15.) Two effects followed this teaching: the astonishment of the people at its quality and method and the arousing of a demoniac who was present in the audience.

A Sabbath in Capernaum

"He taught them as having authority, and not as the scribes." The scribes were wont to speak at second-hand, with the dull and labored citation of the authorities for their statements. Jesus spoke as one who himself knew and understood what he was talking about, with the clarity, directness, and simplicity of such personal knowledge and

35

"Authority" understanding. "Like the prophets, like the Baptist, Jesus interpreted the living, inwardly-speaking God. The scribes interpreted books and traditions." (Bacon.) This appealing contrast, derogatory as it was to the methods of the scribes, pregnant with impending change and threat to cherished scribal leadership, was not likely long to escape their notice or to win their favor. Jesus was unconventional, irregular, unorthodox, measured by their habits and standards. If he remained obscure, uninfluential, he might be ignored. But if he became popular and won any considerable following, he would have to be dealt with as a disturber, a changer of the customs and "the faith" which our fathers have delivered unto us. This situation has not yet developed; but its condition is present, and it will certainly develop with the popularity of Jesus.

Now the synagogue is startled by the cry of a demoniac who recognizes Jesus as "the Holy One of God." But

The De-
moniac
Jesus commands the evil spirit that was in control of the man to be quiet and come out of him; and the command is obeyed with the convulsions and loud cries of the man afflicted.

From one point of view this is an incident in the great controversy between Jesus and Satan and his hosts. It is an instance of his mastery over them, and their recognition of him and his mastery. This inheres in the fact of the cure, and the words of the demon, which apparently had no effect upon the popular estimate of Jesus, and are only the vivid and dramatic phrasing of the fact demonstrated in the cure.

But, of more immediate significance, this exorcism was evidence of Jesus' possession of healing powers and was

36

the basis of great and excited popularity as a healer which threatened to affect profoundly the course of his life and ministry.

When they left the synagogue and went to the home of Simon and Andrew, some of the company informed the Master that Peter's mother-in-law was sick
Peter's Mother-in-Law with a fever; and, in response to this suggestion, he went in and healed her so promptly and completely that she got up and "ministered unto them."

As a result of these two healings, after sunset, when, as good Jews, they might lawfully engage in such work, the friends of the sick and demonized brought them to Jesus for healing, and excited and expectant throngs crowded the street in front of Peter's house; and Jesus healed many of them, enjoining silence, as usual, upon the demons "because they knew him."

Here, then, was an open road to popular favor. Should Jesus take it, and permit his ministry to be transformed
Popularity into a hectic program of healing? Or should he adhere to his purpose to preach the good tidings from God? There seems to have been no doubt in the minds of Simon and the rest: they wanted him to make the fullest use of his healing power and take advantage of the popularity that would accrue therefrom. Not so with Jesus himself. But before day he went out alone into a lonely place to pray; and when the excited disciples found him, he refused to return to the eager crowds and transform his ministry into the type that they desired, but rather proposed to extend his preaching and contest with the demons to other communities. And so

37

"he went into their synagogues throughout all Galilee, preaching and casting out devils" (Mark 1: 39).

The conjunction of these two ideas is of great interest and importance. The emphasis upon preaching the good tidings as against a ministry dominated and determined by works of healing indicates Jesus' own evaluation of his work. The quiet but pervasive influence of preaching, with the change of thinking and of life that would follow its acceptance, was to be preferred to the more spectacular, but at the same time more superficial, method of wonderful works, however worthful they might be in their proper place and use. There is no question here of the actuality of these works of healing; it is a question of comparative values and of method based thereon. And Jesus refused to be diverted into a course of mere wonder-working; and sought, indeed, to evade the curious interest and popular excitement that regularly followed these demonstrations of his power. That explains his repeated commands to those whom he healed not to spread the story of their healing; for the consequent excitement would not help, but would rather hinder, the main purpose of his mission. "Man shall not live by bread alone"; and "Thou shalt not tempt the Lord thy God."

That he should make the casting out of demons something of an exception to this general principle is due to the fact that that particular form of healing was an aspect of his controversy with the Devil, and that each healing at once constituted a victory in that contest and a demonstration of his purpose and power "to destroy the works of the Devil" and break his evil dominion over men.

The wisdom of this decision, and the reason for it, are

38

indicated in the single incident that Mark records of this first preaching tour in Galilee. A leper reverently approached Jesus and with faith besought his cure. "And being moved with compassion"— which was the great motive in his works of mercy—"Jesus stretched forth his hand, and touched him," in defiance, because of pity, of the ceremonial uncleanness thus incurred, "and saith unto him, I will; be thou made clean," thus recognizing, while he ignored, the legal description of leprosy as an "unclean" disease. But when, in response to the healing word, the leper was cleansed, Jesus charged him with great emphasis, even sternness, to say no more about the matter than was necessary for the official establishment and recognition of his cleanness and his consequent restoration to society. And when the man ignored this strange injunction, and spread abroad the story of his healing, so great was the excitement aroused that Jesus could not openly return to Capernaum; and, even in the lonely places which he sought outside the city, great multitudes sought him out, not for his teaching but for the benefits of his healing power.

First Trip

A Hindrance to His Work

And when, after a time, he did venture to return to Peter's house, probably in secret, or as unostentatiously as possible, the very excitement which he had left the city to avoid immediately broke forth again. The scene that follows serves both further to illustrate this point and to introduce a new and ominous development in the life of Jesus. (Mark 2: 1–12.)

Within the house Jesus was teaching those who, having found him, had made their way into his presence, while

39

The Para-
lytic

outside those who could not get into the house filled all the streets, a great and excited crowd.

But a little group bringing a paralytic on a cot, more earnest and persistent than the rest, confident that if they could get their paralytic friend into the presence of the Healer he would be restored, carried the sick man up the outside stairs to the flat roof of the house over the room in which Jesus was, and when they had dug through the clay roofing, or taken off the tiles, let their friend down on his pallet into Jesus' presence, not seeking instruction, but healing.

Jesus was naturally touched by this faithful persistence; but he did not at once grant its implied petition for relief.

Sins For-
given

On the contrary, he said with tenderness to the sick man, "Thy sins are forgiven." These words may have been indicative of intention to perform the cure desired; for the paralysis was probably regarded as a penalty of the sick man's sins, and there was a widespread belief among the Jews that "there is no sick man healed of his sickness until all his sins have been forgiven him." The words are indeed, in form, a mere statement of fact. Alone they may not mean any claim on Jesus' part to forgive, but only that he knows that God forgives, and he imparts that information to the sufferer; and certainly it would be a worthy part of the glad tidings thus to announce forgiveness on this non-legal basis as the divine response to simple faith.

But the scribes who were present do not so understand the words. In their view, they are not a simple statement of the fact that God forgives the sick man's sins, but are an assumption on the part of Jesus of the divine prerogative of forgiveness. They might have objected to the

40

former meaning of the words as ignoring the requirements of the law; but they do actually object to them in the latter meaning as involving blasphemy. And the rest of the narrative proceeds in the light of the correctness of their interpretation.

(2) Thus begins the second stage in these opening events of Jesus' ministry. His period of great popularity as a Healer is followed immediately by the development of acute and permanent hostility on the part of the religious leaders of the people. And Mark has brought together at this stage in his narrative five instances of their criticisms, in order to exhibit clearly the grounds of that hostility which runs through the remainder of the narrative and finally culminates in the crucifixion of Jesus.

Hostility

(a) In the case of the charge of blasphemy (Mark 2: 1–12), Jesus heals the paralytic with a word, "That ye may know that the Son of man hath authority on earth to forgive sins." Certainly it was easier to say, "Thy sins are forgiven," which admitted of no outward test of reality, than to say, "Arise, and take up thy bed, and walk," which must issue in immediate and evident outward result or convict the speaker of pretentious imposture. And if the sickness is regarded as the penalty of sin, which seems to have been the case in the present instance (but see John 5: 14ff.), the removal of the penalty by the cure of the sick would indicate mastery of the cause of the sickness and consequently the authority to forgive the sin, just as the cure of the demoniacs was indicative of the mastery over the realm of the devils. And this is the inference that Jesus would have his critics draw from the incident. But that they did not draw it is apparent from all the rest of the history. Indeed, the natural

"Blasphe-my"

41

and designed conclusion from the scene does not seem to have been drawn by any of those present. The people were, to be sure, amazed; but the nature and authority of the Son of man are submerged, rather than clarified, by this amazement; while for the scribes, who, it will be remembered, were of the sect of the Pharisees, the scene was a ground of offense rather than of commendation.

(b) Jesus now adds another to the four fishermen whom he had already invited to be his followers. In this case his
Matthew choice fell upon a certain Levi, whose surname was Matthew, by which surname he is called in the list of the apostles (Mark 3:18), and which may have been given him by Jesus at the time of his call. (Compare the case of Simon as "Peter," and of James and John as "Boanerges.") This Levi was a collector of customs, probably export duties on the great highway between Damascus and Acre, that then, as now, passed along the northwest corner of the Sea of Galilee not far from Capernaum. Such duties were here levied by Herod Antipas in his capacity as tetrarch of Galilee, and not directly by the Roman authorities; and that fact may have somewhat alleviated the odium of Matthew's occupation. But it is evident that the whole class of publicans to which he belonged was in disrepute among the Jews, especially among the scribes and Pharisees, and Matthew shared in that common disrepute which had now come to attach to the occupation *per se* and not simply to the ill-behavior of the individual who followed it.

Consequently this selection by Jesus of a publican to be one of his intimate associates would have been
"Publicans and Sinners" ground in itself of offense to the Pharisees; but, as a matter of fact, Jesus comprehen-

sively ignored their attitude, not merely in the case of Matthew as an individual, but in regard to the whole class to which Matthew belonged. And not merely in the matter of contacts more or less remote; but he actually went into Matthew's house and ate with him and others of his class, "publicans and sinners," which involved not merely intimacy of association, but the graver offense of table fellowship, with its certainty of ceremonial defilement. (Compare Peter's conduct at Antioch, as described in Galatians 2: 11–21, and the decree of the Council at Jerusalem in Acts 15: 19-21.) For these sinners were defined in terms of legal righteousness, whether ritual or moral, and it was quite certain, whatever might be their moral state, that they would be indifferent to the requirements of ceremonial purity. In any case, they were outside the regular and approved circles of the synagogue, and Jesus' attitude toward them could not meet with approval in the circles of the "pious." Nor would his answer to their criticism seem to them sufficient: for the scribes and Pharisees too, at least some of them, were ready and willing to heal "these that are sick" with the remedies of the law, as they understood, interpreted, and applied it; they, too, were ready to "call sinners" from without their circle, and to conformity to the recognized standards and traditions of accepted "piety." But Jesus' interpretation of righteousness was not that of his critics; and he proposed to call sinners, entering into their midst and associating with them, to a different righteousness from that which his critics professed and would enforce. Hence there could be no adjustment between Jesus and themselves, without a reinterpretation, on their part, of moral values, of religion itself. So long as their standards and their attitude were unchanged, they could only censure Jesus for his irregular and dangerous behavior.

(c) Congenial to the preceding incident, but involving several new elements, is the question of the attitude and **Fasting** practice of Jesus and his disciples in the matter of fasting. This was a religious practice in high esteem among the Pharisees. In addition to the general fasts, the more rigorous (and ostentatious) among them fasted "twice a week"—on Thursday, commemorating Moses' re-ascent of Mount Sinai, and on Monday, commemorating his descent from the Mount. And, in the general practice, though from different motives, John's disciples were at one with them. But Jesus and his disciples, whatever may have been their attitude toward the general fasts—and we may assume that, as good Jews, they observed them—did not conform to the practice of the Pharisees, or to that of John's disciples.

Here, then, was an opportunity not only to criticize him from the standpoint of the Pharisees, but possibly to set up opposition between him and his followers and the teachings and practice of John.

The question now propounded to Jesus, "Why do thy disciples fast not?" might have been raised in all simplicity and earnestness, as this departure from a common and honored religious custom ought fairly to be explained and justified. But it was probably a captious question; and, in any case, it was a point of difference, and as such afforded ground for criticism, and entered into the Pharisaic opposition to Jesus and his work. Whatever may have been the effect upon John's followers, and concerning that we have no information other than may be inferred from their later

44

contacts with Jesus, the effect upon the Pharisees was to widen the breach between them and Jesus.

Jesus' answer falls into two parts:

(1) In particular, he tells the questioners that his disciples have no reason for fasting in the midst of their joy in his presence with them; but that, "when he shall be taken away," there will be reason for fasting, and then they will fast—in which statement he makes fasting an expression of real feeling, and not a mere perfunctory religious exercise. Its meaning and value are not in the act itself, but in the inner attitude of which the act is but the natural and spontaneous expression.

Jesus' Answer

In the second part of the statement Jesus gives the first vague intimation of his death, which, though appearing thus early, is not inappropriate in the light of its setting (compare, especially, Mark 3: 6).

(2) In general, Jesus proceeds to recognize and set forth the incompatibility of his own teaching with the accepted teaching of his day. His spirit and attitude and message cannot be sewed on the old garment of Pharisaic externalism and legalism. This matter of fasting is only a single item, but it is indicative of a great principle. "As a piece of legalism, or asceticism, in which fasting *per se* becomes of moral obligation, it is incongruous with the free spirit of Christianity." For Christianity is not the mere patching of worn-out Judaism; it is something profoudly different in its undertanding and interpretation of God and religion. And this new wine, with the strength of its ferment, cannot be poured into the old wine-skins, stiff and dry and hard, of the current understanding and exposition of the nature and requirements of

New Wine

God. There will be wine-skins to contain it, to be sure; but these wine-skins will be new, fashioned and fit to hold the new wine of the Good Tidings.

Before Mark wrote, Paul had said that believers "are not under the law, but under grace" (Rom. 6: 14); "For Christ is the end of the law for righteousness to every one that believeth" (Rom. 10: 4); "Old things are passed away; behold, they are become new" (2 Cor. 5: 17); "In Christ Jesus neither circumcision availeth anything, nor uncircumcision; but faith working through love . . . but a new creation"(or renewed nature) (Gal. 5: 6 and 6: 15). If any believer of Mark's day wanted to know Paul's authority for these and any similar statements, or why Christians did not observe the Jewish law, he could find his answer in these two parabolic utterances of the Master himself. Christianity was not a reformed and improved Judaism, a new legalism. It was something fundamentally different; and that fact appeared in the life and teaching of Jesus himself, was recognized by him, and was one of the grounds, indeed the single comprehensive ground, of the antagonism of the Jewish leaders that followed the Master through to his crucifixion.

Not Legalism

(d) The fourth and fifth criticisms of the Pharisees both deal with Jesus' behavior on the Sabbath, and hence involve a single principle, illustrated by two incidents and presenting two aspects.

The Sabbath

Beginning with the commandment not to do any work on the Sabbath day, but to remember it and keep it holy, the Pharisees had developed, by process of interpretation and definition, a minute and elaborate system of rules of behavior for the day; and these rules had become a part of their religious standards, supposedly based upon the Scriptures, and important in proportion to the sanctions and importance of the Sabbath day. And naturally they were sensitive to any violation of these rules.

But Jesus violated them, and permitted his disciples to do so, by "working" on the Sabbath; and Mark now introduces two instances of this, the first illustrating what a follower of Jesus may do on the Sabbtah and the second what he ought to do on the Sabbath, with the grounds in each case (Bacon). They serve both as elements in the developing opposition to Jesus and as illustrations of that "new teaching with authority" which was itself a ground of offense to the religious leaders.

The first scene took place in the spring, probably a year after the baptism of Jesus. As Jesus and his companions, among whom were some of the Phari-
Plucking   sees, were walking through the grain fields, the
Grain
disciples pulled off the heads of the grain and ate them. But this was working—"reaping"—on the Sabbath day, and, therefore, "unlawful"; not, indeed, specifically forbidden in the law, but included in the prohibition of work as that was understood and interpreted by the scribes. That Jesus should ignore such a violation of the Law, if he observed it, seemed to the Pharisees thoroughly reprehensible. It alone would brand him as an "unsafe" leader, a radical who ought to be suppressed in the interests of the Church and of religion itself.

And so they brought the matter to his attention: "Why do they on the Sabbath day that which is not lawful?" And to their amazement they found that Jesus not only ignored the act but even defended it, when it was specifically brought to his attention as "unlawful." And the basis of his defense was the simple fact that the disciples were

47

hungry: and one can imagine the Pharisees saying among themselves, "A flimsy excuse, surely." Nor would they be convinced, though they might be silenced, by the form of Jesus' answer.

"David," said Jesus, "when he had need and was hungry, violated the law by eating the shewbread, which only the priests were permitted to eat." That certainly indicates that human need is superior to ceremonial or formal law. But an answer was near at hand in the difference in persons and circumstances, even if so dangerous a principle could be recognized in theory by the Pharisees. What was perhaps excusable in the case of David, under exceptional circumstances, is not to be excused to the common man under common circumstances.

But Jesus' answer does not depend upon David. Hunger and need are hunger and need, whether of prince or pauper; and the act of David was only an illustration of a great and searching principle which Jesus proceeds to enunciate in its application to the present criticism. "The Sabbath," he says, "was made for man, and not man for the Sabbath," whereby the whole emphasis and standard of value is shifted, and any man's simple but real needs are made superior to the formal sanctity and requirements of the Sabbath day. Man is the measure of the Sabbath, and not the Sabbath the measure of man; and the fact that the Son of Man is Lord of the Sabbath does not invalidate this general principle, but rests upon it.

"Made for Man"

If a man may satisfy his own needs on the Sabbath, what shall be his attitude toward the needs of others? If he may "violate the Sabbath" under certain conditions, are there any circumstances under which

Obligation of Service

48

he ought to violate it? These questions are answered in the second incident now related by Mark

Jesus was again in the synagogue. Now he is the object of active suspicion on the part of the Pharisees; and there were some of them (perhaps from the circles of Jerusalem) present watching him, with a view to laying an accusation against him before the Sanhedrin. The occasion of their suspicious scrutiny was the presence in the synagogue of a man whose hand was withered, whose presence might be, indeed, a challenge to sympathy and help, but was for them only an opportunity to watch and criticize the attitude and action of Jesus in regard to him. Jesus' ability to heal the man is taken for granted; and it is regarded as at least probable that he will heal him even on the Sabbath day. But that would be a violation of their law; and on that they proposed to lay their accusation against Jesus.

Jesus evidently knew the delicate, even critical, nature of the situation; but he did not evade the issue, as he might easily have done, and as, under other circumstances, he sometimes did. On the contrary, he accepted the challenge of the situation and, to make the matter as conspicuous as possible, commanded the afflicted man to stand up in the midst of the assembly. In so doing he made clear the difference between himself and the Pharisees and gave them just the opportunity that they sought against him; but at the same time he challenged the allegiance of the people, and gave them the opportunity to choose between himself and his enemies.

While the man thus stood in the midst of the assembly, Jesus asked the Pharisees: "Is it lawful on the Sabbath day to do good, or to do harm? to save a life, or to kill?" There were many things that they might have said in an-

4   49

swer to this question: "It is not ours to judge, we must obey the law and its interpretations"; "To do good is thus to obey"; "There is no question here of doing harm, much less of killing. The man is already afflicted, and we did not do it; and he is in no danger of dying; and if he were, we did not kill him." But they made no answer; and the force of their answer would depend upon their premises, and these were fundamentally different from those of Jesus.

Jesus was grieved, indeed angered, at their spiritual stupidity, that "hardening of their heart" of which Paul speaks in Romans 11: 25—"a hardening in part hath befallen Israel"—and which played so large a part in Paul's explanation of the Jewish rejection of the Messiah. For Jesus, "to do good" was of supreme obligation; "to do good" was to help one's fellow man; and to fail to do good was itself to do harm; not to save a life was itself to kill. And no Sabbath law or sabbatarian practice could set aside this obligation. If there were any difference between the Sabbath and other days in this respect, certainly it could not lie in the fact that the Sabbath should curtail or impair the discharge of this obligation to help mankind. And so, in accordance with this principle, Jesus thus conspicuously healed the afflicted man by the word of his power.

"And the Pharisees went out, and straightway with the Herodians took counsel against him, how they might destroy him." The reason for this attitude of the Pharisees was primarily religious; Jesus did not fit into their scheme of religious values, interpretations, and requirements. Measured by them, he was a dangerous innovator and a heretic; and the continuance and success of his work would jeopardize and finally over-

Plan to
Kill Jesus

50

throw Pharisaic standards and leadership among the people. In the case of the Herodians, the reason was primarily political. Jesus' popularity might easily threaten the public peace; and especially, in some aspect of political Messianism, Jesus might become the head of some powerful movement that would assail the position of Herod Antipas himself. And to the partisans of Herod it might well seem the part of wisdom to forestall such a contingency by the removal of Jesus. And so both religious and political reasons converged in a common, fixed purpose to compass Jesus' death.

51

CHAPTER III

THE CHOICE, TRAINING, AND MISSION OF THE TWELVE

MARK 3: 7–6: 13

THIS purpose of the Pharisees and Herodians to put Jesus to death had important and far-reaching consequences in the subsequent course of his life and ministry.

Consequences

1. He immediately withdrew with his disciples to the shore of the Sea of Galilee, where he would have a safe and ready avenue for further retirement by boat in case the opposition should necessitate such a move. But the fame of his mighty works had spread so widely that great and excited crowds followed him, coming from all quarters of the country. And so great was their eagerness to reach the Healer that Jesus was in

Crowds

danger of physical injury because of their violent crowding upon him, and found it necessary to have a little boat near the shore to keep pace with him, that he might, in case the excitement became too great, take refuge in it from the thronging crowd. For, since he had healed many, and some (doubtless) by a touch, the afflicted had come to the conclusion that all that was necessary for their restoration was to touch the garment or the person of the Healer, and so they crowded to put their hands upon him.

And adding to the confusion and excitement of the scene were the demoniacs, who, "whenever they beheld him, fell down before him, and cried, saying, Thou art the Son of God." This is again an aspect of Jesus' controversy with, and supremacy over, the realm of Satan. But, whatever effect the frenzied cries of these unfortunates may

52

have had on the other hearers, Jesus again commanded them to be silent. He had come to destroy their kingdom, not to confirm or establish his own upon their testimony. Such a situation would have compromised his position, and might even have lent color to the later charges that he cast out demons by Beelzebub, the prince of the demons.

2. Jesus had purposed, from the beginning of his ministry in Galilee, to enlist others in his work, as is indicated in his words to the four whom he first called to be his companions, "Come ye after me, and I will make you to become fishers of men" (Mark 1: 17). But now a condition has arisen which makes larger and more definite organization imperative. Such a scene as the one just described, coupled with the threat of the leaders against his own life, calls for immediate provision for the multiplication of Jesus' activities and the perpetuation of his work.

Choice of the Twelve

And so Jesus now selects, from the larger company of his disciples, twelve (according to the traditional "twelve tribes of Israel"), who are to be his intimates and his agents in the expansion and preservation of his work. They are (1) to be with him, for more adequate instruction; (2) to go forth to preach; and (3) to have authority over the unclean spirits. In other words, after a period of preliminary instruction, they are to take up the distinctive work of Jesus himself in preaching and in overthrowing the kingdom of Satan.

In this little company, which was the only organization formed by Jesus in his lifetime, and which was the depository of his message for the future, it is well to note:

(a) That there were eleven Galileans and one Judean— Judas, the "man of Kerioth," who proved the traitor.

(b) That all of them whose station in life we know belonged to the same social group to which Jesus also belonged.

(c) That the number contained one of the despised class of the publicans (Matthew), whose presence in this inner circle could only be an offense to the stricter Jews.

(d) That the number contained also one of the radical or militant party of the nationalists and Messianists (Simon, the Cananæan, or the Zealot), whose presence might attract popular favor in certain, especially Galilean, circles, but might also bring upon the group the suspicion of a violent Messianic program.

(e) That most of the group play little or no active part in the further development of the narrative, Peter, on the one hand, and Judas, on the other, playing the chief parts in the later life of Jesus.

The composition of this first and only group of Jesus' intimates throws considerable light upon his own attitudes and upon the nature of the movement in which he and they are engaged. He is of the common people, and he finds his friends among them. His mission is especially and increasingly to the unchurched masses, the lost sheep of the house of Israel, for whom the leaders cared but little, who were, indeed, the lost sheep because of the indifference and misleading of those who should have been their guides. Jesus is their *tribunus plebis*, the champion of their place and rights in the household of God, from which they have been, in effect, excluded by the religious interpretations and demands of the scribes and Pharisees. And since these leaders have no sympathy, but only opposition, for his movement, it must be carried on, as for, so through the common people.

Their Status

And this isolation of Jesus is further emphasized by the interlocked incident of the action of his family and the judgment of the scribes who had come down to Jerusalem to look into his work.

When his family heard of Jesus' intense activity, and the popular excitement and official opposition that he was causing, they came to the conclusion that he must be mad, "beside himself"; and so they set out to take charge of him and put him under restraint. While they are on the way, the scribes who came down from Jerusalem passed a similar, but harsher and more specific, judgment upon him. They said: "He hath Beelzebub, and by the prince of the demons casteth he out the demons." This adverse judgment of the scribes from the center of the religious life of the nation at once shows the solidarity of the official opposition to Jesus, and is ominous for his future. It is no small and insignificant provincial group to which he is unacceptable; it is the religious leadership of the nation that is against him, and he can hardly look for a better understanding or more generous treatment if he moves nearer to the heart and center of that leadership.

Charge of the Scribes

But Jesus meets their criticism directly and conclusively. If it be true that his activity is that of Beelzebub, then, since his activity is a consistent impairment of the range and power of Beelzebub, there is an anarchy in Satan's own kingdom. It is in process of self-destruction and must soon come to an end; and that very fact is evidence of the truth of Jesus' message: "The kingdom of God is at hand." But if the criticism of the scribes is untrue, and Jesus' activity is not that of Beelzebub, then it must be true that one stronger than Satan is making a successful attack upon

55

his kingdom, and the very success of this attack confirms the message: "The kingdom of God is at hand."*

In fact, and in particular, Jesus' assault upon the kingdom of Satan is due to the presence of the Holy Spirit with him, as is evidenced by the very nature of the enterprise; and for any one to call this Holy Spirit "an unclean spirit" is to blaspheme against this Holy Spirit, and to incur the condemnation and the penalty of such blasphemy. It is a fatal perversion of the moral judgment, a hopeless confusion between the good and the bad.

The Holy Spirit

Jesus' family now appears before the door of the house, and sends in to summon Jesus that they might restrain him from his work. But when the word was brought to him of their presence and summons, Jesus takes occasion to declare a newer and higher relationship than that of flesh and blood. The doers of his Father's will are his true kindred; and if his fleshly kin fail at this point, the fleshly relationship must give place to the higher relationship to the Father that transcends the fleshly. And so Jesus lays the basis for a new relationship in the family of God, based upon a common devotion to the Father's will.

Jesus' Family

3. Now, too, a change took place in Jesus' own ministry in response to the situation in which he found himself. It will be observed:

(a) That, while the choice of the Twelve is related in Mark 3: 13–19, their mission is related only when we reach 6: 7. The intervening section, therefore, belongs to the first purpose of their call, "that

Concentration

---

*Unless, indeed, one should say that Beelzebub craftily yields a little with a view thereby of gaining more.

56

they might be with him," and is devoted to their training for their later mission.

"After Mark 3: 6," says Burkitt, "a new era in the ministry is opened. From that moment begins the separate existence of the embryo Church. From that moment the aim of Jesus is not the rousing of the multitudes, as it had been hitherto, but the instruction and training of his own disciples. True, a crowd still follows him on occasion, and sometimes he is willing still to teach. But if he does so it is by way of an exception, because they have come to him from a distance and he will not send them away without a word." (Gospel History, 81.)

The opposition of the leaders is thus met by a concentration of Jesus' work. It is no longer as free and general as it had been in its initial stages, but is largely limited to a smaller group, and, in the section we are now considering, is especially directed to the inner group of his twelve intimate associates.

(b) A corresponding change, also, takes place in the method of his instruction; for "he taught them many things in parables, . . . and without a parable spake he not unto them" (Mark 4: 2, 7, 34).

Use of Parables

And he adopted this mode of teaching partly as a factor of safety and partly as a method of sifting out his hearers. In the parable something of a veil was drawn over his teaching. As a consequence, those who were already actively hostile could less easily lay hold upon his words; and those who were merely curious, and not earnest seekers for the meaning of his message, would soon become indifferent or be repelled by a form of teaching that required of them insight and further search. What is not easily understood is soon dropped and ignored by the

57

superficial and the careless. They have a chance to see; whether they see or not depends upon their attitude toward their opportunity; and thus the presentation of the opportunity is itself a sifting and a judgment.

By this sifting and judgment through the use of parables, (1) the religious leaders and the majority of the Jewish people were, under the judicial hardening of God, Their Purpose rejected by him, and thus excluded from participation in the coming Messianic kingdom; at the same time and by the same process, (2) a righteous remnant was selected and secured that should inherit the kingdom prepared for it from the foundation of the world.

This rejection of Israel was therefore not total. Neither was it final; for this veiling of the truth was only temporary and provisional. "Is the lamp brought to be put under the bushel, or under the bed, and not to be put on the stand? For there is nothing hid, save that it should be manifested; neither was anything made secret, but that it should come to light." (Mark 4: 21, 22.) So, in due time, the truth that was now hid in parables for the sifting of Israel should be made plain, and the uncovered lamp would lighten all the house.

But meantime this sifting process gathers out the righteous remnant that constitutes the group of the disciples who are now sharply marked off from the rest of the people. "Unto you," says Jesus, in specific contrast to "them that are without"; and Mark adds, "without a parable spake he not unto them; but privately to his own disciples he expounded all things" (4: 11, 34).

To this group, thus selected, and centering in the Twelve, Jesus now devotes his main attention. His public contacts and activities do not cease, but the developments

58

Training of the Twelve of the ministry have drawn a line between his enemies and his friends, and his chief interest now lies in the instruction of the latter in the mystery of the kingdom which he had to impart.

The instruction that follows, between the calling and the mission of the Twelve, falls into two parts, differing in form and to some extent in theme. The first part consists of a group of three (or four) parables, selected from a much larger number, and dealing with certain aspects of the kingdom (4: 1–34); while the second consists of a group of four mighty works, emphasizing the lesson of faith, and demonstrating the comprehensive and supernatural power of Jesus.

By Parables The three parables that Mark has selected for record at this point are evidently chosen in view of the situation in which Jesus now found himself. They all deal with the central theme of Jesus' preaching, the nearness of the kingdom of God; but they deal with it not in relation to the nature of the kingdom, but in relation to its nearness and the mode of its coming. And they are all designed to answer certain questions relative to this coming, which the situation would inevitably raise and make urgent in the minds of the disciples.

Faith "How is it that the preaching of the kingdom receives such scant response?" That question is answered in the parable of the sower. As the farmer does not get fruit from all the seed he sows, so the sower of the Word need not expect a perfect harvest. The yield depends not alone upon the sower and the seed, but upon the receptivity of the soil in which the seed is planted. Nevertheless the farmer sows, and though some of his seed is wasted, from the receptive soil he gathers abundant and compensating harvest. One need not therefore be surprised at the obduracy of the Jewish leaders from the hard soil of whose hearts Satan snatches away the seed as soon as it is sown, nor at the superficial and fruitless receptivity of other hearers of the Word. All this was to be expected. It is enough to know that there is also the good ground, and that in it the seed will yield its fruit.

"But if, indeed, the kingdom is near, why does it not immediately appear? Why this delay?" This question is answered in the parable of the patient husbandman, who sows his seed, and with patient confidence awaits the certain harvest. Since the seed is good, and "the earth brings forth fruit of itself," he knows that, at the proper time, there will certainly be the harvest and its reaping. There is nothing more that he can do to hasten that time; but he can with patience and with confidence wait for it.

Patience

"But can the kingdom come without observation, without dramatic inauguration, initial prodigy? Can this little group be its beginning, the promise of its great realization?" This question is answered in the parable of the mustard seed. It grows, according to its nature and in due time, from tiny seed to great herb. But grow it does; and no man who plants the mustard seed is either discouraged because of its smallness, or disappointed because the great plant does not appear at once.

Understanding

So Jesus now reaffirms in parables, with especial view to the situation which had arisen at this stage of his ministry, and for the comfort and confirmation of the disciples in view of that situation, the message with which he had opened his ministry, "The kingdom of God is at hand."

60

The use of the figures of growth in all three parables is significant. Burkitt, indeed, sees in the idea of the *growth* of the kingdom "the mystery of the kingdom of God," which is imparted to the disciples but hidden from those who are without that circle. And certainly the idea of slow, vital processes preparing for, and in a sense introducing, the kingdom, is very different from the program of violence and revolt of Messianic agitators of the Zealot type, and introduces a novel factor when compared with apocalyptic expectations of the sudden and cataclysmic inauguration of the kingdom by immediate and miraculous intervention of God. But the period of growth in each case is short and does not impair the message of the nearness of the kingdom, and the idea of an initial period of growth does not eliminate apocalyptic suddenness at the end, when the harvest is ripe (in the first two parables) and the reaping takes place.

Growth

What Jesus chiefly intends to impart to his disciples in view of the stress of the situation is (a) the certainty of the coming of the kingdom, despite small beginnings, obscurity, and opposition, and (b) patience in waiting for it, despite its (brief) delay—for it is "at hand."

Lessons

4. Jesus had chosen the Twelve "that they might be with him, and that he might send them forth to preach, and to have authority to cast out demons" (Mark 3: 14). They were to preach the nearness of the kingdom, and the teaching in parables which we have just studied had particular reference to that aspect of the work they were called to do. But they were also to have authority to cast out demons, that they might play their part in the spread and success of Jesus' conflict with these unseen powers of evil. And

61

so, with particular reference to this aspect of their work,

By Miracles Jesus now performs a series of miracles which (a) demonstrate his power in this field and (b) teach the great lesson of the necessity and power of faith. His words of encouragement are sustained by demonstrations of his power, so that the question concerning him becomes increasingly not "What is this?" but "*Who* is this?"

(a) Immediately after the teaching in parables, Jesus, worn with the strain of the day, commanded the disciples to set out, in the boat from which he had been teaching, for the eastern side of the Sea of Galilee. As they went, a sudden storm fell upon them, a storm of demonic origin,

The Storm sent by the prince of the power of the air (Eph. 2: 2), and the disciples were greatly frightened. In their terror they awoke the Master, who was quietly sleeping in the stern of the boat; and Jesus "rebuked the wind, and said unto the sea, Peace, be still," and they obeyed him, "and there was a great calm."

Then Jesus reproved the disciples for their lack of faith. They should have known by this time that he was Master of the demons, that no demoniac agency could injure him or his. How could they enter into his conflict with the demons, if any demoniac manifestation could thus reduce them to a panic of fear? Such faithlessness would deprive them of all "authority to cast out demons." If they would take up that work, they must believe in the adequacy of the power at their disposal for its accomplishment. Otherwise they were defeated in advance.

But the disciples were now filled with a new fear because of the manifestation of supernatural power which they had just witnessed, a timid and anxious awe in the presence of one who possessed such power. And in this fear they raised among themselves a question of the identity of Jesus that played an essential part in the further unfolding of the narrative. "*Who then is this*, that even the wind and the sea obey him?" Whatever views they had thus far formed of Jesus were evidently inadequate, and would have to be revised. "Who then is this?" This question

" Who Is This?"

receives no specific answer at the time, but it lies in the background, and soon comes to the front again in several quarters, and, for the disciples, finds its answer later in Peter's confession at Cæsarea Philippi, "Thou art the Christ." Indeed, the whole of the following narrative is of the nature of an answer to this question.

(b) When they arrived on the eastern side of the sea, the little company was met by a man acutely and distressingly possessed by a multitude of demons. The

The De-moniac

number and malignity of these demons is indicated partly by the man's own statement and his behavior under their control, and partly by the size and behavior of the herd of swine into which they were permitted to enter (for animals as well as men might be occupied by the demons). But, despite their number and power, these demons too recognized the authority of Jesus as "the Son of the Most High God," and his power to make them do whatever he would. And this is the main purpose in the recording of the incident. The scene of the miracle, in Gentile territory, and the number and violence of the demons, show most clearly the area and completeness of Jesus' mastery over them.

But the crowds that gathered upon the spread of the news of the miracle, when they heard and saw what had been done, "were afraid," as the disciples themselves had been afraid at the stilling of the tempest. In both cases

63

the "fear" was due to the supernatural power manifested in the acts of Jesus; but in the case of these Gerasenes this fear was both intensified and modified in character by the impression that this power might be hurtful as well as beneficent. The demoniac was healed, indeed; but the swine were destroyed; and it was this destructive element in this manifestation of the power of Jesus, with its possible consequences, that centered their interest and determined their action. They could not tell what "harm" such power might do, and so, lacking assured confidence in its uniform beneficence—for did they not see the dead swine? —they respectfully but urgently requested Jesus to leave their territory.

Jesus acceded to this request. But in his going he left among them a commissioned witness to his mercy. For he would not allow the restored demoniac, in his gratitude, to attach himself to his person; but ordered him to remain behind and tell his friends what God in his mercy had done for him. And so this restored demoniac, in Decapolis, became the first commissioned witness of the power and mercy of God as manifested in Jesus: "and he went his way and began to publish in Decapolis how great things Jesus had done for him; and all men marveled." And so the good tidings found an evangelist in the territory of the Gentiles.

(c and d) The two mighty works that follow, the healing of the woman with the issue of blood and the raising of Jairus' daughter, may be regarded as also aspects of Jesus' controversy with Satan and his hosts of demons, partly because of the frequent reference of sickness to demoniac agency, and partly because, in the case of another woman who had "a spirit of infirmity," Jesus

64

specifically describes her as one "whom Satan had bound" (Luke 13: 10–16), while in regard to death it was a part of his work to "bring to naught him that had the power of death, that is, the devil" (Heb. 2: 14), and "the last enemy that shall be destroyed is death" (1 Cor. 15: 26).

But this interpretation does not appear in the Marcan narrative (nor in the parallel accounts of Matthew and Luke). The incidents are, indeed, additional demonstrations of the power of Jesus, but their emphasis is not so much upon that power as upon *Faith* as the condition of the reception of its benefits. And so the incidents reach back to the stilling of the storm, with the reproachful question to the disciples, "Have ye not yet faith?" And they reach forward to the rejection of Jesus and his message at Nazareth, where Jesus' own beneficent activity was limited because of the unbelief of the villagers. Thus there is implied a duality of faith. The representatives of the Master must have it for the doing of his work; and those who would receive his benefits must have it as the condition of this reception. The former aspect is to the fore in the scene on the lake, the latter in the two miracles of healing that are now related.

Power of Faith

When Jesus returned to the western side of the lake, to the vicinity of Capernaum, a certain ruler of the synagogue there (who "was intrusted with the care of public worship, including the appointment of readers and preachers"), Jair (Jairus) by name, approached him with reverent earnestness, and begged him to come to his house and restore to health his little daughter who was at the point of death.

Jairus' Daughter

Jairus' request indicates his confidence in the ability of Jesus to do what he asked, and thus throws light upon

5
65

Jesus' established reputation as a healer. Men might account for his power in friendly or in unfriendly fashion, but the fact of the power was acknowledged by friend and enemy alike; and such was Jairus' affection for his little daughter, and such his sense of need, that he would enlist Jesus' power, despite the fact that Jesus was already in disrepute with the class to which Jairus belonged.

This confidence that Jesus could and would grant him his heart's desire—for this was Jairus' "faith"—was subjected to yet greater stress as Jesus went with him toward his home. For some one from Jairus' household met them on the way with the information that the little girl was dead, and so there was nothing more to be done. "Why troublest thou the Teacher any further?" may also reflect the repugnance of the household to the reception of Jesus. Certainly it indicates the conviction that the child was dead, and that Jesus, whatever his power with the living, could do nothing with the dead; and thus, in the sequel, it serves to set off both the power of Jesus and the faith of Jairus.

Jairus' confidence might well be shaken by this news; but Jesus encouraged him with a word, "Fear not, only believe." And so they went on, leaving the crowd behind and taking with them only Peter and James and John, who here first appear as constituting the innermost group of Jesus' most intimate friends. And when they reached the house everything confirmed the message of the child's death that had been brought them on the way, for the place was already noisy with the weeping and the wailing of the hired mourners, who, when Jesus, entering the house, said to them, "The child is not dead, but sleepeth," laughed him to scorn. This, again, may be a reflection of the attitude of the household to Jesus; but, in any case, it indicates the conviction that the child was dead, and that only mourning was now appropriate.

When Jesus had driven the hired mourners out of the house, he took the parents of the child and his three disciples, and went into the room where the body
Raised was laid out. "And taking the child by the hand, he saith unto her, Talitha cumi [one of the very few Aramaic phrases that the Gospels preserve]; which is, being interpreted, Damsel, arise. And straightway the damsel rose up, and walked [indicating the immediacy and completeness of her restoration]; for she was twelve years old [and able to walk]. And he commanded that something should be given her to eat"—which indicates both the tender thoughtfulness of Jesus, and the completeness of the girl's restoration to life; she could both eat and walk; no phantom, then, and no sort of delusion.

Naturally, the beholders of this scene "were amazed with a great amazement," and that seems to have been its only immediate result. But Jesus, in keeping with his usual practice, enjoined silence upon them to avoid increase of the popular excitement with its overemphasis upon his powers as a healer and its interference with his higher work of preaching and teaching the word of the kingdom. Such popular excitement might also inflame the anger of his opponents, particularly of the Herodians, and give them further grounds for charges of a popular Messianic disturbance. But Jesus' power over "the last enemy" was demonstrated, and the fact was left in trust with three chosen witnesses; and with and by that fact not only did Jairus' faith have its reward, but the power of faith was certified to all who thereafter might call upon Jesus.

But another demonstration of the power of Jesus, and the power of faith, had been given as Jesus was on the way to Jairus' house. For in the throng that had **The Afflicted Woman** set out with him had been a woman with a long-standing and apparently incurable issue of blood. She, too, having heard of Jesus' mighty works, now turned to him as a last resort for her own healing. But not openly; rather, she said, "If I touch but his garments, I shall be made whole." And so she made her way to him, unnoticed in the crowd, and reaching out her hand touched his garment; and immediately she was cured of her sickness.

But Jesus, "perceiving in himself that the power proceeding from him had gone forth," in response to this touch of faith—for it evidently was not called forth by the common touch, for the throng was crowding him—singled out the woman, and, when she had told him all, dismissed her with the tender words, "Daughter, thy faith hath made thee whole; go in peace, and be whole of thy plague." These words only confirm the fact already accomplished; the woman's healing had taken place before the words were spoken.

Thus the emphasis is thrown upon faith, not only in these words of Jesus but in the whole narrative. The **Faith** power that inhered in Jesus flowed out, without any deliberate activity on his part, simply in response to this woman's faith. It did not respond to the common touch, but it did respond immediately and effectively to the touch of faith, and Jesus himself knew that it was the touch of faith because of his immediate consciousness of the efflux of the responding power. The power, indeed, is there. One might say that it is emphasized by this representation of its inherence and its immediate, unpremeditated manifestation. And this doubtless is a part of what Mark means to teach. But the fact remains that the power responds, and so its presence is made manifest, only and here solely, in response to the attitude and act of faith. Without that, whatever the nature and extent of the power, it would have remained latent in Jesus, its presence undemonstrated and unknown. Faith, therefore, and faith alone, is here the master key that unlocks the store of power in Jesus.

(e) This section on the training of the disciples is fitly brought to a close by the story of Jesus' rejection at Nazareth, "his own country" (Mark 6: 1–6a).

Rejection at Nazareth

For in it we see most vividly the isolation of the group and the difficulties that would attend the further expansion of the work. Criticism, opposition, unbelief, had appeared elsewhere in Galilee; now they appear even in the Master's "own country." What, then, might his disciples expect? And if unbelief at Nazareth limited Jesus' own ability to do there any mighty work, their activity in his name might well be limited by the same attitude of those to whom they might come to minister.

Jesus is not excluded from the synagogue, and not yet wholly descredited therein. For on the Sabbath of his visit to Nazareth, when he went into the synagogue, he received and accepted the invitation of the ruler of the synagogue to speak to the assembled people. But the most of his hearers were not disposed to take him seriously or to give him a respectful hearing. What he said, and the reports of his mighty works, seemed to them incongruous with what they knew of his family and station in life. For an ex-carpenter, of lowly family, Jesus seemed to be playing

69

an altogether too pretentious rôle. "The picture," says Gould, "is of several groups of objectors, of which one throws out the sneer, 'Whence to this one these things?' another takes it up in the same tone, 'And what is the wisdom given to this one?' and a third exclaims, 'And such miracles done through his hands!'" And so "they were offended [that is, "caused to stumble"] in him."

Jesus, hearing their criticisms, or seeing their attitude reflected in their behavior, said to them, "A prophet is not without honor, save in his own country, and among his own kin, and in his own house," in which words we may see one phase of the more friendly popular estimate of Jesus, as "a prophet" (see below). Several of the early commentators saw in them, also, an anticipation of the transfer of the gospel from the Jews to the Gentiles; and it is in this view that Luke places the incident at the beginning of his Gospel, which, taken with its companion work, The Acts of the Apostles, unfolds the powers and processes of this transfer.

The fact that here at Nazareth Jesus "could do no mighty works," because of the unbelief of the people, presents the obverse of the story of the healing of the woman with the issue of blood, just recorded. If in her case his power was elicited by faith, here, where faith is lacking, his power is limited by that lack—not, indeed, in the abstract, but in its manifestation. And so here he could only lay his hands on a few sick folk and heal them, the few who, presumably, had the faith that was indispensable to the manifestation of the power.

Grieved and marveling because of their unbelief, Jesus left Nazareth and "went round about the villages teaching," accompanied still by the disciples.

5. Now the time had come to intrust the disciples with the work for which they had been chosen. They had been taught by parable and mighty work the mystery of the kingdom and the power of faith, and they were now to deliver and demonstrate that message to others.

The account of their mission is very briefly related in Mark (6: 7–13, 30), and the most of that brief narrative is taken up with the instructions that Jesus gave them as he sent them out. Except in one particular, these instructions deal only with their manner of life. They are to make no special preparation for their journey, and to take nothing with them against to-morrow and its needs. For their simple sustenance they are to depend upon the generous hospitality of the people to whom their message is to be delivered; and should this hospitality fail in any place, they are to indicate on leaving that place that those who have refused to receive them have no part or lot in the message of the kingdom which they are preaching.

They "preached that men should repent," in preparation for the coming kingdom, thus carrying forth the initial and central message of Jesus. "And they cast out many demons." In view of the statement just before their specific charge, "he gave them authority over the unclean spirits" (6: 7; compare 3: 15), it is probable that this was a specific item in Jesus' instructions; and it is a further indication of victory in that conflict with the powers of evil of which mention has been made above. "And anointed with oil many that were sick, and healed them"—where the healing ministry is described not in terms of the practice of Jesus but of the practice of the later Church (Jas. 5: 14).

"And the apostles gathered themselves unto Jesus, and

71

told him all things, whatsoever they had done, and whatsoever they had taught." (Mark 6: 30.)

This summary treatment of the apostles' mission avoids any distraction of attention from the activity of Jesus himself. And yet the fact of the mission must be recorded, partly as the completion of the call of the Twelve, and as exhibiting an aspect of the activity and plans of Jesus, and especially because of the effect of the mission upon his subsequent career.

72

CHAPTER IV

THE CRISIS AND CONCLUSION OF THE WORK IN GALILEE

MARK 6: 14–7: 13

"AND Jesus went round about the villages teaching. And he calleth unto him the twelve, and began to send them forth by two and two." Thus there were now seven lines of ministry reaching out in different directions in Galilee.

The chief result of this enlarged activity was to bring the name of Jesus conspicuously to the attention of Herod Antipas, the tetrarch of Galilee and Perea. He may have heard of Jesus before; but now his name had become well known through the activity of the apostles as his representatives, preaching and healing in his name, as well as through the activity of Jesus himself, as he went round about the villages teaching. And this very activity exhibited Jesus now as the head of an organized and systematically expanding movement, which would add no little, and no little of danger, to Herod's interest in him.

Result of the Mission of the Twelve

About the time of the apostles' return—perhaps the cause of that return—Herod had at last put the imprisoned John to death. Mark traces this murder back to the anger of Herodias at John's uncompromising censure of Herod's conduct with her, and says nothing of any other factor in the crime. But Josephus says that Herod's act was due to his fear that John might become the leader of a Messianic insurrection. In either case (or both), the story of the forerunner's death.

Death of John

73

related by Mark between the mission and the return of the apostles, is indicative of danger to Jesus at the hands of Herod, especially since now, as the head of an organized and expanding movement, he himself might very well be suspected of planning a Messianic revolt that would throw the country into turmoil and threaten Herod's security and place. And those Herodians who had already taken counsel with the Pharisees how they might put Jesus to death would scarcely miss this opportunity to prompt Herod to put the worst construction upon the present organization and expansion of Jesus' work.

There were, indeed, distinct Messianic intimations in the reports of Jesus that were brought to Herod. For some said (as in R. V., margin) that John the Baptist was risen from the dead, "and therefore do these powers work in him." "But others said, It is Elijah. And others said, It is a prophet, even as one of the (great ancient) prophets." Even this vaguer designation of Jesus as a great prophet might have its Messianic content, for the reappearance of prophecy was to be one of the signs of the approach of the Messianic era. The supposition that he was John, risen from the dead, is probably related to the supposition that he was Elijah— the difference between the two suppositions lying in the directness of the supposed relationship of Jesus to Elijah. One group ignored John in this matter, and regarded Jesus as Elijah directly; the other group saw Elijah in John, Elijah's fate in John's death, and Elijah's—that is, John's— resurrection and reappearance in Jesus. For there was not only the simple expectation of the reappearance of Elijah, but a more elaborate expectation according to which he should reappear, be put to death by the ruling tyrant,

Who Is
Jesus?

74

and then reappear again through his resurrection; and this more elaborate form of the expectation may underlie the identification of Jesus with the risen John the Baptist.

In either case, in the mention of Elijah we see not merely a reflection of the impression of greatness that Jesus made upon his contemporaries, but a specific Messianic content in that impression because of the common belief that Elijah would reappear as the forerunner of the Messiah. If Jesus were this Elijah, whether directly, or as the John-Elijah risen from the dead, then the Messiah must be at hand—a conclusion that, however welcome to the common people, would not be welcome to Herod and his court.

John had performed no miracles. But in the more elaborate Elijah-expectation that prophet, when he rose from the dead, would perform many, as the means of inaugurating the Repentance which should precede and prepare for the coming of Messiah. Jesus was performing many miracles; and it was on the ground of these wonderful works that the conclusion was reached that he was John the Baptist (*i. e.*, Elijah) risen from the dead.

Herod's View This view of the matter was adopted, in part at least, by Herod himself. If he adopted the whole of the more elaborate expectation, then he would be the ruling tyrant who had put Elijah to death, and by so doing had unwittingly forwarded the coming of the Messiah; and that is possibly reflected in the peculiarly emphatic form of his statement, "Whom *I* [emphatic] beheaded, John, this one is risen from the dead." In which case, his words are not the expression of a conscience stung by the execution of the wilderness prophet, but are the expression of surprise and fear at the part, and the folly of the part, that he had unwittingly played in forwarding the

75

very Messianic movement which (according to Josephus) he sought to check, and which, if unchecked, would cost him his throne and his life. Certainly, Herod's belief that Jesus was the risen John did not make him a follower of Jesus, or even tolerant of him. Rather it intensified and concentrated upon Jesus all of Herod's hostility to the Messianic movement, and from this time on Herod's territory, Galilee and Perea, became so unsafe for Jesus and his work that he found it wise to withdraw therefrom.

And this danger was enhanced by Jesus' very popularity with the people, which was now at its height. For when the apostles returned to him—probably gathering again in Capernaum—they were so thronged with eager crowds that again (as in Mark 3: 20) they had no opportunity even to eat. Such a situation was not without its dangers as well as its difficulties—danger from Herod, especially as his attention is now particularly directed to Jesus; **Dangerous Popularity** and danger from the Pharisees, who were always offended at the popularity of Jesus; and danger, too, even from the crowds, whose enthusiasm for his mighty works not only tended to shift the emphasis from his teaching, but might at any time break forth, especially with the Messianic suggestions in their evaluation of him, into actual Messianic insurrection. So difficult was it to minister to the lost sheep of the house of Israel.

And so Jesus again sought retirement with the disciples by crossing the Lake in their boat to the eastern shore— **Retirement** which was outside the territory of Herod Antipas. But even so he was unable to escape the crowds, for they outwent him around the edge of the Lake and met him when he disembarked on the other shore. There Jesus, "having compassion on them, because they

76

were as sheep not having a shepherd" (does this reflect John's recent death?), devoted the rest of the day to their instruction. Of the "many things" that he taught them concerning the kingdom of God no record has been preserved, unless, indeed, we are to find something in the narratives of the miracles with which the day was closed.

These miracles are two: the feeding of the five thousand— which is the only miracle recorded in all of the four Gospels —and the walking on the sea in the night that followed— which is omitted by Luke, but appears in the other three Gospels.

When the late afternoon came on, and the disciples suggested to Jesus that the crowd should be dismissed in order that they might go and buy themselves something to eat, Jesus said to the disciples, "Give ye them to eat." And when he had ascertained that there were five loaves and two fishes in the company, he took them, and, blessing and breaking, had the disciples distribute them to the whole multitude, which had been seated in orderly fashion on the grass to receive the food thus provided. "And they all ate, and were filled. And they that ate the loaves were five thousand men. And they [the apostles] took up broken pieces, twelve basketfuls, and also of the fishes." (Mark 6: 42-44.)

5,000 Fed

Just after this miracle, Jesus "constrained"—that is, compelled, forced—the disciples to enter the boat again and set out for Bethsaida Julias, which was a little way from the shore on the northeastern side of the Lake, and still outside of the territory of Herod Antipas. He himself remained behind to dismiss the crowd, and after that was done withdrew alone

Walking on the Sea

77

into the mountain to pray. Then, "about the fourth watch of the night," which was from three to six o'clock A.M., seeing the disciples still toiling on the wind-tossed sea, Jesus came out to them, walking upon the water. And when he had calmed their fears—for they thought they were seeing a ghost—and had entered into the boat with them, the wind miraculously ceased. "And they were sore amazed in themselves; for they understood not concerning [*i. e.*, "by reasoning built upon"] the loaves, but their heart was hardened" (6: 51, 52).

These two miracles are recorded primarily to exhibit the (tenderness and) supernatural power of Jesus; and it is

Purpose of
the Miracles

perhaps significant that in the synoptic narratives the record of such miracles of power over the inanimate world is practically, if not altogether, confined to this period of the crisis in Galilee, when the question, "Who is Jesus?" is acute not only in the minds of the disciples but with the people and the court. Such miracles do not, indeed, answer that question; but they contribute to its answer. For they indicate that, whoever Jesus was, he was certainly no whit less than the greatest of the ancient prophets, and might, therefore, be even greater than they. If Moses and Elijah and Elisha had been given power over the waters in ancient days (see Exodus 14: 22, 15: 25, 17: 5; 1 Kings 18: 41; 2 Kings 2: 8, 2: 14, 2: 19, 6: 6) and power for the miraculous increase or provision of food (see Exodus 16: 4ff.; 1 Kings 17: 9; 2 Kings 4: 1–7, 5: 1–19), much more did Jesus possess such power, and demonstrate it in these mighty miracles.

And these miracles throw another light upon the crisis in

Power

Galilee, and the apparent failure of Jesus' ministry there, as well as the tragic issue of his

78

death that soon followed. For one possessed of such power could not be defeated if he were minded to use his power in his own defense. His apparent defeat could be brought about only because he voluntarily refrained from using such powers as were clearly at his disposal.

The feeding of the five thousand, moreover, is connected with that popularity of Jesus with the people which was so large a ground for official opposition to him.

Excitement The intensity of excitement and enthusiasm for Jesus caused by that miracle is reflected in Mark's strong expression that Jesus "compelled" the disciples at once to leave the scene. And one might fairly infer, even without appeal to the statement of John (6: 15), that this excitement had a Messianic content, which was not pleasing to Jesus, and from which he would desire to separate first his disciples and then himself. But the walking on the water was private, a demonstration to the disciples only of Jesus' power, the meaning of which seemed afterwards so plain that the then obtuseness of the disciples could only be accounted for on the ground that "their hearts were hardened."

Though the disciples had set out for Bethsaida, on the northeastern edge of the Lake, they came to land, for some reason not given, at the plain of Gennesaret on the western shore, which was again in the territory of Herod Antipas. Here Jesus moved about in an area not specifically described, and for a time, probably brief, in the midst of the wildest excitement of the people; and the miracle of healing by touch alone, as in the case of the woman with the issue of blood, was repeated many times, for "as many as touched him were made whole."

Whether because of this new outburst of popular excite-

ment, or because of Jesus' return to their vicinity, the
local Pharisees, in company with certain of the
Hostility of scribes who had come down from Jerusalem,
the Phari- now sought Jesus out to interview him about
his mode of life and teaching. We have seen
how, on a previous occasion, the local Pharisees went out
and took counsel with the Herodians how they might put
Jesus to death (Mark 3: 6). Between that ominous scene
and the present interview they have dropped out of sight;
and we have no information as to what they were doing in
the interval. Scribes who came down from Jerusalem
have, also, come before us as drastic critics and opponents
of Jesus, when they passed on him the judgment that he
was possessed of Beelzebub and by the power of this Prince
of Demons performed his exorcisms (Mark 3: 22); but they,
too, have not appeared since that encounter.

We cannot tell whether the group that now comes to
Jesus is composed of the persons already described or
consists (in part) of a new delegation from Jerusalem; but
we may be sure of the continuity of antagonism and mur-
derous purpose, and we should infer from the sharpness of
Jesus' treatment of them that they have not been idle
during this period of silence. And now, just as we may see
the hostile activity of the Herodians in the court's anxious
and menacing interest in Jesus, so we may see in this visit
of the Pharisees and the Jerusalemite scribes the reappearance of their part in the compact between the religious and
political leaders to do away with him. Either because the
time now seemed opportune, in view of the interest of the
court, to bring the issue to a crisis, or because Jesus'
popularity, and the excitement attending his activity, were
now so great that it seemed imperative to take some deci-

80

sive action, the local Pharisees and the scribes, representative of the prestige and authority of the party in Jerusalem, seek this interview with Jesus, "not [as Bede says] to hear the word, but solely to stir up questions of controversy," with a view to breaking his hold upon the common people and somehow compassing his destruction.

There was, indeed, ample material for controversy, as we have already seen; but the point immediately before their eyes, indubitable and sufficient, was the fact that Jesus' disciples, without rebuke from him, ate their food without previously washing their hands to remove any possible ceremonial uncleanness.

Washing of
Hands

"For the Pharisees, and, indeed, all the Jews [that is, all the strictly orthodox Jews], except they wash their hands diligently [*i. e.*, with the fist], eat not, holding the tradition of the elders," says Mark, in parenthetical explanation of the situation.

From the beginning of Jesus' ministry, his teaching had created no little surprise because "he taught them as having authority, and not as the scribes" (Mark 1: 22). Here that difference appears again and is at once illustrated and brought to an issue. The scribal teaching was based upon "the traditions of the elders" as final and determinative for Jewish orthodoxy—those "traditions of the fathers" to which Saul, the Pharisee, had devoted himself with such unexampled zeal, as he says in Galatians 1: 14—those teachings of prominent and influential rabbis that constituted a body of precedent, doctrine, practice, starting, indeed from the written Law, and professing the greatest reverence for it, but dealing with it in formal, legalistic spirit, and thus developing a new code parallel to and even superseding the

Jesus vs. the
Scribes

6   81

Law from which it started. It was, as Paul saw after his conversion, a code of the letter that killeth and not of the spirit that maketh alive. It wholly missed the tremendous and abiding significance of the prophetic movement and spirit, with its forward look and creative impulse, and was the concrete and supreme expression of "the narrow finality of Judaism."

The question of the scribes and Pharisees, "Why walk not thy disciples according to the tradition of the elders, but eat their bread with defiled hands?" raised, on the basis of the specified particular, the whole issue of the attitude of Jesus toward the tradition of the elders. And so Jesus' answer falls into two parts, the first dealing with the whole matter of the tradition and the second taking up the immediate application of the principle to the case of eating with unwashed hands.

The tradition, says Jesus, which these scribes and Pharisees teach as their doctrines is, in fact, merely "the precepts of men," and is not only not in accord with the mind and requirements of God, but is actually repugnant thereto and sets at naught some of the finest elements of that divine revelation with which the chosen people had been intrusted. And so in their devotion to their tradition, as Isaiah (29: 13) had said, "This people honoreth me with their lips, indeed, but their heart is far from me"; for they "leave the commandment of God, and hold fast the tradition of men."

The Traditions

The tradition made a distinction between duties to God and duties to parents—a distinction which cannot properly be made—and said that in case of conflict arising between such duties, which is in fact impossible, the duty to God should take precedence over the duty to parents. Consequently, if a man has vowed any or all of his substance or his earnings to God, "The scribes say, 'The vow cannot be cancelled, nor the earnings withdrawn from the temple treasury, even to save the man's aged parents from destitution'" (Bacon). And so the divine obligation to honor one's parents, including filial ministration to their physical needs, may be set aside by the operation of some supposedly higher obligation. But there is in fact no such higher obligation, as is both written in the commandment and implanted in the nobler impulses of the soul; and to suppose such higher obligation is to make void the word of God in Scripture and in the soul by your traditions, which ye have delivered—doctrines which are but the precepts of men, and not the word of God.

"And many such like things ye do," concludes Jesus, gathering up and comprehensively repudiating the whole body of the tradition of the elders that pos-
Repudiated sessed the characteristics of the instance which he has cited. And thus he gives in most vivid form an indication of the fundamental difference in the content of his teaching from that of the scribes and Pharisees. For Jesus, the obligations of humanity, of man to man in loving, helpful, generous service, according to capacity and according to need, are of the very essence of religion, are, in themselves, of their very nature, duties to God which may not be ignored or superseded. But the scribes had some other and higher duties to God, whose center was conformity to priestly ritual, ceremonial, and ecclesiastical requirement. Their claim to superiority to other men and preference in the divine esteem was not based on a more generous and more fraternal attitude toward their fellow men, but rather on such things as fasting twice a week and giving

tithes of all that they possessed. And they would not learn the simple but revolutionary lesson that God requires mercy rather than sacrifice.

This part of Jesus' answer seems to have been directed immediately, and apparently privately, to his questioners. For he now "called to him the multitude again," and took up with them the matter of eating with unwashed hands.

And he said to them in a "parable," "Hear Real Defilement me all of you, and understand; there is nothing from without the man that going into him can defile him, but the things which proceed out of the man are those that defile him."

Those words seem plain enough to us, and their teaching simple and natural enough, because we have come to think of God and his requirements in some degree at least as Jesus did. But for the original disciples these words needed explanation. It was not plain to them that the Master could mean exactly what these words imply. And so when they had entered the house, they asked Jesus privately for an explanation of the parable; and he, grieved at their slowness to understand, made it very plain to them that defilement is not a matter of eating and drinking, but of the state of the heart, out of which are the issues of life. "Whatsoever from without goeth into the man cannot defile him. . . . That which proceedeth out of the man, that defileth the man."

"This he said, making all meats clean"—and the fourteenth chapter of Romans will indicate the need of such a lesson in the Roman Church—a revolutionary "All Meats Clean" lesson, indeed, in the light of the food requirements among the Jews both in the Law and in the tradition of the elders, doing away at a single sweep

84

with the religious obligation and value of all those requirements and making defilement altogether a matter of the moral condition of the inner man.

In this whole controversy Jesus was teaching with authority and not as the scribes, repudiating comprehensively the tradition of the elders, which they so much magnified, and even some of the laws from which that tradition started its long and tortuous course, and setting forth, in lieu of scribism, a fundamentally different conception of the nature of God and the requirements of religion. Between such diverse and antagonistic attitudes and interpretations there could be no peace; and it is not strange, therefore, rather it is dramatically appropriate, that this scene should bring to a close the Galilean ministry of Jesus. He had no more place in those parts.

Withdrawal
from Galilee

85

CHAPTER V

WITHDRAWAL FROM GALILEE

MARK 7: 24–8:26

AND so Jesus withdrew from Galilee. His work there was done. He had, indeed, won great popularity with the masses of the people, but mainly as a healer of their diseases; and his popularity was as full of peril as of promise. It could only be used, in its crude and excited form, as a political asset, for preparation and support of a Messianic revolt. Unless one were ready thus to capitalize it, popularity of this sort, attended by such widespread and hysterical excitement, might of itself necessitate a withdrawal from the scene, lest the popular enthusiasm should sweep its object into its own channel, and the situation thus become the master of him who had created it.

But, side by side with this popularity, and in large measure in consequence of it, Jesus had aroused the implacable hostility of the religious and political leaders in Galilee; and, unless he was prepared to lead the people against these leaders, it was no longer safe for him to stay there. The lines of hostility that had appeared in his earlier ministry had converged upon an irremediable situation. The Court of Herod was watching Jesus with active suspicion and anxiety, and he had finally and definitely broken with the religious leaders. He must either use his popularity for his own protection, or he must withdraw from the territory dominated by his enemies.

Reasons for Withdrawal

And so he withdrew from Galilee, partly for safety and seclusion, and partly for meditation upon the situation and

86

Route
the determination of his future course in the light of it. In his withdrawal he left not only the territory of Herod Antipas but Jewish soil entirely, and betook himself first northwestward into the Gentile territory of Tyre and Sidon—Syrophœnicia—and thence eastward, around the northern borders of Galilee, and down again to the eastern shore of the Sea of Galilee; all this while outside the jurisdiction of Herod Antipas and the area of any effective influence of the scribes and Pharisees.

Thus beyond the territory dominated by his enemies, he was, at least comparatively, safe from their plots for his destruction. But if personal safety were to become the determinant of his future course, only three alternatives were open to him: (1) He must abandon altogether the work that he had begun; or (2)

Problem
he must change its scene; or (3) he must change its form and purpose. And, in the last case, he might either try to come to terms with his enemies, or he might put himself at the head of a popular movement for their defeat. But if the idea of personal safety should be minimized or ignored, then, of course, the whole field would be open to him.

It has been already indicated that Jesus' power was not limited to Jewish territory. That is now more specifically demonstrated by a series of miracles performed among the Gentiles.

(a) He came into the borders of Tyre and Sidon; "and would have no man know it; but he could not be hid." For a certain woman, whose Gentile status Mark

**The Syrophœ-
nician
Woman**
is careful to emphasize—"Now the woman was a Greek [or Gentile], a Syrophœnician by race"—hearing of his presence (see 3: 7),

87

hunted him out and besought him to heal her little daughter who was possessed of a demon.

Here, then, is importunate faith among the Gentiles. What will Jesus do in the light of it? His answer indicates, with apparent harshness, that the time of the Gentiles is not yet come. His first responsibility is to his own people —he is sent to them. Later, the Gentiles also may be the partakers of his bounty, "to the Jew first, and also to the Greek," as Paul says in Romans 1: 16.

But the woman's distress cannot wait; she needs help. And so, while she recognizes the priority of the Jew, she claims, even as a Gentile house dog (for "is God the God of the Jews only? is he not the God of Gentiles also?" Rom. 3: 29), a present share in the crumbs that fall from the children's table. And for this answer Jesus grants her petition, and, though he has not seen and does not see the child, assures her that "the demon is gone out of thy daughter," which the mother finds to be the case when she returns to her home.

Hence we see that Jesus' power is effective, even at a distance, on Gentile territory. "On Jesus' dealings with **The Lesson** Gentiles, compare Matthew 8: 5–13, where also there is a cure from a distance. To St. Paul the Gentile gods are demons (1 Cor. 10: 20), and the Gentile world is subject to powers opposed to God (1 Cor. 8: 5); so that the story before us must have appeared to Gentile Christians prophetic of the emancipation of the heathen by the salvation, which appeared first among the Jews, from the tyranny of irrational and evil powers."* But we see, also, that while the individual Gentile may be the beneficiary of Jesus' compassion and power, and while

---

*Menzies, "The Earliest Gospel."

there is forecast a time when his gospel shall be for the Gentile as well as for the Jew, for Jesus himself his mission and responsibility were toward his own people, and he will not ignore that fact to transfer his activities to the Gentiles.

(b) When Jesus reached the eastern side of the Sea of Galilee, the friends of a deaf man, who had also an impediment in his speech, brought him to Jesus, with earnest request for his healing. In the account of how this request was granted we have mention of details that are generally lacking from the records of his other cures (but **The Deaf Stammerer** compare the next cure of the Marcan record, 8: 22–26). Jesus takes the deaf stammerer away from the crowd, touches his ears and his tongue with a finger moist with spittle, prays with uplifted eyes, and says to the man, in Aramaic, "Ephphatha" (meaning "Open"), and immediately his hearing was restored and the defect in his speech corrected. The several steps here described—the isolation of the man, the touch, the employment of spittle, the prayer—were stages in the concentration of the man's attention and the awakening of his faith, so that the miracle belongs with the other faith-healings which we have already noted.

Jesus sought to keep the miracle quiet, in accordance with his usual practice; but here again his injunctions to secrecy were useless: "But the more he charged **Popular Approval** them, so much the more a great deal they published it." As a consequence, there was profound astonishment among those who heard and saw, and they gave voice to most comprehensive and significant commendation: "He hath done all things well; he maketh even the deaf to hear, and the dumb to speak."

89

This is the highest and most specific commendation that the people have yet given to Jesus, and it is probably for this primarily that this incident is here recorded. The demons, indeed, have recognized Jesus from the first as "the Holy One of God." The leaders of the people have taken just the opposite view. But among the common crowds, spectators of his mighty works, there have been progressive expressions of opinion. At the first miracle in Capernaum, "they were all amazed, saying, What is this? a new teaching! With authority he commandeth even the unclean spirits, and they obey him." (Mark 1: 27.) At the cure of the palsied man, "they were all amazed, and glorified God, saying, We never saw it on this fashion." (Mark 2: 12.) In the definitions precipitated by Herod's interest, there was a general agreement that he was a prophet, whether the risen John, the returned Elijah, or "as one of (ancient) prophets." (Mark 6: 14–16.) But now, not only does this judgment of the crowd (in Gentile territory, but probably upon the lips of Jews) differ from the harsh judgment of the leaders in Galilee, but it con-

Is This the Messiah? tains a definite Messianic implication. For it is a reminiscence of two Messianic passages in Isaiah: "And in that day shall the deaf hear the words of the book, and the eyes of the blind shall see out of obscurity, and out of darkness" (Isa. 29: 18); and, "Then the eyes of the blind will be opened, and the ears of the deaf shall be unstopped" (Isa. 35: 5). The idea is the same as that more simply expressed in the parallel in Matthew: "And all the multitudes were amazed, and said, Can this be the son of David?" (Matt. 12: 23.) In a word, the Messianic implications which we have seen in the prophetic

90

evaluation of Jesus have now advanced to the point where the people are thinking of his works of mercy, if not quite in terms of his own Messiahship, certainly in terms of the expected Messianic era; and these two terms, if separated, lay close together.

(c) Perhaps it was this Messianic idea that caused a new crowd now to attach itself to Jesus and follow him for a distance from their homes into some remote and lonely place on the eastern side of the Sea of Galilee; or, perhaps, crowds already gathered had followed him without regard to distance or to comfort; but, at any rate, at the close of three days of such enthusiastic following "Jesus called unto him his disciples, and saith unto them, I have compassion on the multitude, because they continue with me now three days, and have nothing to eat; and if I send them away fasting to their home, they will faint on the way; and some of them are come from far." (Mark 8: 2, 3.) As a consequence, he proceeded to feed them, as he had previously done in the case of the five thousand, out of the scanty provisions—seven loaves and a few small fishes—which constituted the disciples' store. And thus he demonstrated again both his compassion and his supernatural power, a power directed by compassion and used for the relief of the simplest needs of men.

4,000 Fed

The effects of this miracle are not described. But as soon as Jesus had sent the crowd away—it numbered about four thousand—he and his disciples got into the boat and crossed over "into the parts of Dalmanutha," which, though not certainly located, apparently lay on the western side of the Sea, and probably not far from Capernaum.

These incidents of the wandering in Gentile territory

91

not only have indicated the comprehensive area and nature of Jesus' power, but they have brought to the surface certain vague Messianic ideas in the minds of the people. They have shown, also, that Jesus will not abandon his work, and that, though it might be carried on in Gentile territory, he will not transfer his activities to that field. And the present return to Galilee apparently contemplates the resumption of his work there.

But the only incident that Mark records of this visit to Galilee indicates the impossibility of such a course. The conditions that had brought about Jesus' withdrawal some days or weeks before had not changed in his absence. For the Pharisees, as if they had been lying in wait for his return, came to him and demanded of him a sign from heaven, by which his authority might be vindicated and his further activities justified. They made a proposal to Jesus, it seems, that if he would give them such a certifying sign, they would cease their opposition and receive him and his message. Only let him show them some apocalyptic sign, like the darkening sun or the falling stars, presageful of the early coming of the kingdom which he preached, and he would be safe, and free to carry on his work to "success." But if Jesus could not, or would not, give them such a sign, and still persisted in working among his own people, he must count on their growing hostility and must weigh and face its consequences. That, at least, is the temptation that they presented to him— specious, indeed, and treacherous, too; for there is no reason to believe that anything that Jesus could have done would have led them to an acceptance of himself and his gospel. But this, certainly, Jesus, being Jesus, could not

Resumption of Work in Galilee Impossible

"Show Us a Sign"

do; for it would have involved a fatal and final denial of all that he was and all that he stood for.*

And so, with a sigh, he told them that no (such) sign should be given them. If his words and deeds and himself

No Sign

were not sign enough of the justice of his cause and the truth of his message, no sign of a different order should be granted to that generation. The demand for such a sign, even if honest, indicated a profound misunderstanding of Jesus; and the granting of that demand would not remove, but only confirm, that misunderstanding. If that was the condition of the resumption of his work in Galilee, there was nothing left for him but to withdraw; and so he and his disciples forthwith reëntered the boat and returned to Gentile territory on the northeastern shore of the Sea.

Their departure seems to have been quite hasty—a "flight," as Burkitt describes it; for in their haste to get away the disciples forgot to take any bread for the trip, and found themselves with only a single loaf in the boat.

After they put to sea, Jesus warned them to beware of the leaven of the Pharisees and the leaven of Herod, meaning (1) partly the hostility and consequent dan-

---

*Menzies has an admirable note on this point. He says: "There are two points settled in Jesus' mind against which the demand for a sign deeply offends. First, he has made up his mind not to employ any sensational or presumptuous method in advancing his cause (see 'fishers of men,' 'sowers,' 'physician,' etc.); and, secondly, he is convinced that the advent of the kingdom is not in need of any signs, but carries its own evidence with it to every one whose eyes are open. The kingdom has announced itself and is a thing of the present; to ask a sign of its coming is to relegate it to the future, and to ask for respite from its claims." ("The Earliest Gospel": Mark 8: 11.)

"Beware of the Leaven" ger that had already developed in those quarters, since wherever the Pharisees and the Herodians appear together they appear as enemies of Jesus and plotters against his life, and (2) partly, especially in the case of the Pharisees, that attitude of mind, that understanding of religion, that lay behind their enmity and had just found expression in their demand for a sign from heaven as a certificate of Jesus' status and authority. The disciples are to beware of their danger; but more, if they themselves are to understand Jesus and be faithful to him, they are to beware of that attitude from which the danger sprang.

But Jesus' warning was misunderstood by the disciples. Because he spoke of the "leaven of the Pharisees and the leaven of Herod," and because their minds **Misunderstanding of the Disciples** were at the moment occupied with the thought of their lack of bread, they supposed that he spoke of literal bread and was warning them not to expect it or seek it from these groups, but to provide their own supply. As if he had said, "You need not look for bread from the Pharisees and the Herodians; and if you should get it, you would better be careful not to eat it. You must bring your own bread." And so they saw in Jesus' words a comment on the unprovisioned condition of the boat, and a reproof of themselves therefor, and they said, "It is because we have no bread" (R. V., margin).

Jesus was grieved at their misunderstanding, especially in regard to the most fundamental aspect of his warning. To lay so much stress upon physical bread, to be themselves disturbed and to think that he was concerned about it, ought to have been impossible in the light of the two feedings of the multitudes that they had but lately witnessed. Was not this, indeed, to miss the meaning of his mission and his message as badly as the Pharisees themselves had missed it? Must they, too, have "some sign from heaven"? Was not their daily experience filled with signs that were plain enough and convincing enough to the open mind and receptive heart, signs truly from heaven to those who had spiritual insight and sympathy to read them rightly? "Why reason ye, because ye have no bread?" says Jesus; "do ye not yet perceive, neither understand? Have ye your heart hardened? Having eyes, see ye not? and having ears, hear ye not? Do ye not yet understand?" Clearly they needed warning against the leaven of the Pharisees and of Herod; for how could they face its issue as danger unless they were purged of its contamination as blindness and misunderstanding?

The miracle that Mark now records, as Professor Bacon points out, is peculiarly appropriate in the light of this

The Blind Man Healed

situation. When the little company reached Bethsaida (Julias), near the northeastern shore of the Sea, again in Gentile territory and outside the zone of immediate danger, a blind man was brought to Jesus with request for healing by his touch. And here again, as in the case of the deaf stammerer, Mark describes the isolation of the man, for Jesus "took him by the hand and brought him out of the village," and the stages and processes by which at last his sight was restored, "and he saw all things clearly." It would appear that the confusing influence of the crowd, and the sluggishness of the man's faith, made his healing slow and difficult. And nothing could more vividly and dramatically illustrate the condition and needs of the disciples themselves. They were still like the deaf stammerer, "having ears, they heard not," and like this blind man, who, "having eyes, saw not." They had, indeed, been separated from the multitudes. They could, perhaps, already speak with stammering tongues, and see men as if they were trees walking. But they were not yet in full possession of their faculties; and, because their faith was sluggish and their understanding meager, their healing was a slow and difficult process.

No immediate result of this healing of the blind man is recorded, if we ignore Jesus' now familiar effort to avoid publicity by the injunction, "Do not even enter into the village." But, just as the healing of the deaf stammerer had been followed by the expression of Messianic ideas on the part of the people, so this present miracle is immediately followed in the narrative by the eliciting of a specific Messianic confession on the part of the disciples, and the difficult teaching concerning the nature and issue of that Messiahship that was necessary for the clarification of the idea, so that, by and by, they might both "speak plainly" and "see all things clearly." In other words, the whole of the preceding section, beginning with the withdrawal from Galilee (Mark 7: 24) and closing with the healing of the blind man (Mark 8: 26), serves as a preparation for, and a transition to, a new stage in the life and teaching of Jesus.

He is determined not to give up his work, not to modify it in conformity to the expectations and demands of the Pharisees, and not to change the field of his activities to the Gentiles. His last encounter with the Pharisees has made it clear that Galilee is no longer open to him, unless he is prepared to court an untimely death and thus leave his mission to and for the lost sheep of the house of Israel unfinished; for as yet he has not pre-

Conclusion

sented himself to the seat and center of the nation's religious life and its ills, Jerusalem. In this situation, there is but one thing that he can do. Shut out from Galilee, he must go to Jerusalem, and, going, must take the consequences.

What those consequences are apt to be is already clear to him, but it is equally evident that his disciples are by no means ready to face and accept them. They needed new and yet more difficult instruction, in view of the situation that had now arisen, to prepare them, as far as possible, against the crisis into which that situation would rapidly unfold. And that instruction Jesus now proceeds to give them.

7

CHAPTER VI

THE DOCTRINE OF THE CROSS

MARK 8: 27–9: 29

As a preliminary step in the new and difficult instruction that Jesus now had to impart to his disciples, he here for the first time deliberately raises the question of the identification of himself. "And Jesus went forth, and his disciples, into the villages of Cæsarea Philippi: and on the way he asked his disciples, saying unto them, Who do men say that I am?" All vague and unformulated opinions are now to be clarified and brought to concrete expression and committal in this little group of his chosen friends. All hitherto unanswered questions concerning his identity and status, whether within their group or without, are now to receive, for them at least, their answer. This is a necessary point of departure, a background and bulwark, for the revolutionary teaching that is to follow.

Who Is Jesus?

In answer to Jesus' question concerning the popular estimate of himself, the disciples told him that he was commonly regarded as a prophet, recounting the opinions that we have already heard expressed in connection with Herod's interest in him (Mark 6: 14–16). But this popular judgment, interesting and significant as it is, does not go far enough for present needs. And so Jesus makes his inquiry more personal and searching: "But who say ye that I am?" And Peter, answering for the group, said: "Thou art the Christ [*i. e.*, the Messiah]." The formulation and expression of this conviction, with the committal that it

The Messiah

98

involved, was what the Master sought. It is not yet to be made public; but it is to serve, with the disciples, as the starting point and presupposition of the revolutionary reinterpretation of the Messianic idea that underlies all the rest of Jesus' life and teaching.

The central point of this reinterpretation was the doctrine of the cross—that the Christ (Messiah) must suffer.

The Cross And now, then, for the first time, Jesus tells them plainly of the tragedy that awaits him— him whom they have just specifically acknowledged as the Messiah—of rejection and of death, a tragedy lightened, indeed, but not for them, by the then unintelligible promise of the resurrection from the dead.

How novel, unacceptable, and inconceivable this idea was is indicated by their reception of this its first enunciation. A prophet might, indeed, be rejected and put to death: that had happened both in former times and in their own day. But nothing of that sort could possibly happen to the Christ, simply and sufficiently because he was the Christ. His career must be one of personal triumph, directed toward, and issuing in, the nation's deliverance from its oppressors. And so Peter took Jesus aside "and began to rebuke him" for entertaining and expressing any such notion of his Messianic career and destiny.

And doubtless here, as in his previous confession, Peter expressed the general opinion of the disciples. Certainly

A Stumbling- the cross was a "stumblingblock" not merely
block to Jewish opponents of the Pauline gospel, but to them because they represented the common attitude of the Jewish people—an attitude which had at first been shared even by Jesus' own most

99

intimate Jewish friends. And that, not only naturally, but perhaps inevitably. For all their Messianic traditions and hopes, based upon and buttressed by the triumph and deliverance passages of their Messianic prophecies, had gathered around a heroic and victorious figure, who should dash his enemies in pieces as a potter's vessel, set up again and occupy the throne of David, and thus "restore the kingdom unto Israel." Such passages as the Suffering Servant passages of Isaiah had not come into their own; rather they were obscured and smothered by passages of quite a different sort. It is, indeed, as hard for us now to realize the depth and strength and color of the current Messianic expectations of the days of Jesus as it was for the disciples then to accept the new and revolutionary conception that Jesus at this point began to present to them. There was a way across through the resurrection, partly as vindicating the gospel of the cross, partly as opening the way for a second coming; but at present this way is closed to the apostles, as the mention of the resurrection did not remove, but only increased, their perplexity. No wonder, then, that Peter and the rest could not at first receive this new teaching. Indeed, the conflict between their ideas and those of Jesus on this matter underlies all the rest of the narrative of Jesus' activity, and it was only finally resolved for them by their confident conviction of the fact of his resurrection.

Nevertheless, this idea of rejection and the cross, difficult and revolutionary as it appeared, was fundamental. And so Jesus sharply rebukes Peter, in words **Peter Rebuked** that remind us of the response to the third temptation in Matthew, when he said to the Tempter, who was offering him the kingdoms of this world in return for an act of worship, "Get thee hence, Satan; for it is written, Thou shalt worship the Lord thy God, and him only shalt thou serve" (Matt. 4: 10). Peter, in his repudiation of the doctrine of the cross, is dominated by the same sort of worldly ideals to which Satan had there appealed. He is, indeed, Satan's mouthpiece, for he is not thinking in terms of God's values and purposes, but in the common terms of men. "Get thee behind me, Satan," says Jesus to him, "for thou mindest not the things of God, but the things of men."

And then Jesus proceeds to declare that this gospel of the cross is not for him alone, but for all those who would really be his disciples. If they would share his rewards, they must also know the fellowship of his sufferings, becoming conformed unto his death (Phil. 3: 10). "If so be that we suffer with him, that we may be also glorified together" (Rom. 8: 17). His disciples must, therefore, arm themselves with the same mind, that mind that was in Christ Jesus. They might not repudiate the cross, whether for their Master or for themselves. On the contrary, "If any man would come after me, let him deny himself, and take up his cross, and follow me." Only by losing the life that now is—*i. e.*, by a resolute readiness to lose it—can they enter into the better and more glorious life that is to come.

A Teaching for All

But to repudiate this divine principle, to be ashamed of a crucified Christ and of his teaching of a fellowship of suffering—to take, for their Master or for themselves, that attitude and scheme of values that Peter had just taken—this would leave them uncovered and desolate in the crucial hour of the coming of the Son of Man, for he will then be

For a Place in the Coming Kingdom

ashamed of those who are now (and because they are)
ashamed of him. Nor is this hour so remote as to be
devoid of effective meaning. On the contrary, "There are
some here of them that stand by, who shall in no wise
taste of death, till they see the kingdom of God come with
power." (Here the participle "come" is not present,
"coming," as of an event in process, but perfect, "having
come," as of a result attained and abiding. There were
some among Jesus' auditors who should see the kingdom
of God not merely coming, but actually come.)

This statement reverts to the initial summary of Jesus'
preaching given in the opening verses of our Gospel
(Mark 1: 14, 15): "Now after John was delivered up,
Jesus came into Galilee, preaching the gospel of God, and
saying, The time is fulfilled, and the kingdom of God is at
hand: repent ye, and believe in the gospel." "The
kingdom of God is at hand," so close, indeed, that some
of Jesus' companions (not, necessarily, of his disciples)
should see it realized.

Jesus and his companions were living in the last days
of an era, an epoch in the history of the world and the
race, which Paul calls "this present evil age"
(Gal. 1: 4), and which the disciples describe
in one of the endings of Mark's Gospel as an "age of law-
lessness and unbelief, under the dominion of Satan"
(compare 2 Cor. 4: 4). "But the night is far spent, and
the day is at hand" (Rom. 13: 12). A new and better
era is about to begin, the era of the kingdom or the rule
of God, when the dominion of Satan shall be broken, and
the kingdoms of this world shall become the kingdoms of
our God and of his Christ. And so near is the dusk of the
one epoch to the dawn of the next that some of those living

Near

102

among the companions of Jesus should see and participate in the passage from the one epoch to the other.

The induction of the new era was conceived and expressed in current apocalyptic terms. It was not commonly regarded as a process of evolution or of growth (but compare the growth parables of Jesus), as the new unfolding out of the old by some inner power of transformation, retaining and enhancing the good and depressing and eliminating the evil of the old order. It was rather a sudden and cataclysmic process, a divinely wrought revolution, whereby, sharply and suddenly, by divine intervention and not at all in the ordinary course of things, the old order was brought to an end and the new initiated. This is reflected in the clause, "When the Son of Man cometh in the glory of his Father with the holy angels."

Apocalyptic

In Mark's Gospel this coming of the Son of Man is closely connected, but not identical with, the destruction of Jerusalem and the temple and the tribulation and ruin of those distressful days. "But *in those days, after that tribulation*, the sun shall be darkened. . . . And then shall they see the Son of Man coming in clouds with great power and glory" (Mark 13: 24–26). This national ruin is a part of the coming of the kingdom of God with power, and so Professor Bacon says: "We cannot do honest justice to the unbroken consensus of primitive testimony without acknowledging that Jesus pointed his disciples to the expected intervention of God, which should be the vindication of his gospel, before the generation which heard and rejected it should have passed away. The sublime faith in God which ventured this declaration was indeed justi-

Destruction of Jerusalem

fied by the event. The kingdom of God did come with power. The city which 'knew not the time of her visitation, and rejected the things which belonged to her peace', did undergo a frightful 'judgment.'"*

But in the connection immediately before us, the chief purpose of these sayings concerning the coming of the Son of Man and the coming of the kingdom of God with power is to enforce the main theme of the section in which they occur, the difficult and unpalatable doctrine of the cross, by the assurance of the certain and early demonstration of its validity and worth.

The disciples stumbled at this doctrine because, among other things, it subverted all their ideas of the dignity and glory of the Messiah. To remove this difficulty, a revelation was given to three of their number—Peter, James, and John—in the vision of the Transfiguration of Jesus; the single purpose of which was to confirm their Messianic confession, despite what seemed to them the un-Messianic way of the cross upon which they were now entering.

The Transfiguration

The scene of this revelation was an unnamed "high mountain," commonly identified with Mount Hermon, which lay some miles to the northeast of Cæsarea Philippi. And the revelation contained three factors, all converging upon the common end of demonstrating the Messiahship of Jesus:

(a) Jesus himself was transfigured (Greek, "metamorphosed") before them, and they were permitted to see, for a moment, the real Jesus in the celestial body of his glory. His earthly house of this tabernacle was dissolved, and he appeared in that build-

Its Lessons

---

*"Beginnings of Gospel Story," on Mark 9: 1.

ing of God, not made with hands, eternal in the heavens. Certainly they should understand, then, that the Jesus of humiliation and the cross, their earthly Friend and Master, was more than appeared to common human eyes, and could not be confined to the categories of those who were thinking merely in the terms of men and not in the terms of God.

(b) "And there appeared unto them Elijah with Moses: and they were talking with Jesus." But Elijah and Moses, prophet and lawgiver, were the most commanding and revered figures of their religious history, and were, in popular tradition and expectation, the witnesses of the Messiah. Their appearance, therefore, in friendly converse with Jesus is enough to indicate that he and they are not in controversy; and that, not only in general, but especially now in the light of his new teaching on the way of the cross (compare Luke 16: 29–31, especially 9: 31). But more than this: as the expected witnesses of the Messiah, their appearance made specific the identification that was only inferential in Jesus' transfiguration, and confirmed, by two unimpeachable witnesses, the fact of his Messiahship.

(c) And last of all, wondering and sore afraid, the chosen three were permitted to see the cloud of Jehovah's presence (compare Ex. 16: 10; Lev. 16: 2; Num. 11: 21; and elsewhere), "which was expected to reappear in Messianic times" (Swete), and, as it overshadowed them, to hear His voice, speaking out of its depths and saying, "This is my beloved Son: hear ye him." And in that last command the end of the revelation finds expression. Jesus is, indeed, the Messiah, by confession, and now by overwhelming demonstration; but confession and demonstration alike are meaningless and ineffective unless they issue in acceptance of Messiah's teachings and obedience to his words, however strange they may seem to us and repugnant to our common modes of thinking and principles of behavior. And this, too, is of particular pertinence to the new doctrine of the cross.

Moreover, it is Jesus who is the "Beloved Son," and neither Moses nor Elijah. They might bear their witness; but, great as they were, they were subordinate. "Hear Him" It is not they whom the disciples are commanded to hear: it is Jesus. The Law, indeed, was given by Moses; but grace and truth came by Jesus Christ. God had of old time spoken unto the fathers in the prophets, by divers portions and in divers manners; but now he hath spoken unto us in his Son. Therefore we ought to give the more earnest heed to the things that were heard, lest haply we drift away from them. And it was this very motive of the singularity and supremacy of Jesus, in the Transfiguration scene, that was to lead the disciples to this same more earnest heeding of his words. They were to see in Jesus one higher than the law and the prophets, the single and supreme object of their loyalty, and were to pass over into new modes of thinking and of life in keeping with this richer apprehension of their Master. He, and he alone, was the beloved Son: him, therefore, henceforth should they hear.

But the vision actually had no such revolutionary effect. It confirmed, indeed, their confession of the Messiahship of Jesus; but it did not lead them to accept his interpretation of that Messiahship. In the gospel of the cross, in particular, they were still not willing to "hear him"; but their old ideals of the things of men, on which

106

their hearts were set, still ran at cross purposes with these new ideals of the things of God which Jesus was trying to impart. And so, sadly and strangely enough, the Transfiguration was practically without effect on the subsequent course of the life of Jesus.

What the effect might have been if the revelation had been made public at the time, we cannot tell; for, for some reason, apparently in accordance with his usual policy of avoiding needless and spectacular publicity, Jesus commanded the three disciples, as they came down from the mountain, not to make their experience known until after his resurrection from the dead. What he meant by such a resurrection they did not then understand, and continued to discuss its meaning among themselves. They knew, of course, of "the resurrection at the last day" (John 11: 24), but what sort of an individual resurrection this might be that was to serve as a dating point for subsequent acts of theirs, that they did not understand. But the injunction to silence was plain enough, and their obedience to that injunction accounts for the fact that this revelation did not come to the knowledge of even the body of believers until some time after the event.

"Tell It Not"

There was, also, a very pertinent question in the minds of the disciples as they came down from the mountain. They were familiar with the popular expectation—probably shared it—that Elijah should come before the coming of the Messiah. And yet here they were confessing Jesus as the Messiah, and receiving a great revelation confirming that confession; but what of Elijah, where was he? And so they said to Jesus, "How is it that the scribes say that Elijah must

Elijah to Come?

107

first come?" To which Jesus answers that the opinion of
the scribes is here correct; but that, as a matter of fact,
Elijah has already come; meaning to say—though he
does not here use the name as does the Gospel of Matthew
(17: 13)—that they are to see the expected Elijah in John
the Baptist and his work and fate.

But, he goes on to say in substance, your question
carries with it other implications that you ought not to
ignore. The scribal opinion and the popular expectation
of the coming of Elijah are based on the prophecy of
Malachi (4: 5). If you accept that prophecy, and are
actually looking for the Elijah there predicted, why do
you ignore those other prophecies that speak of the
Suffering Servant of Jehovah, so that you are unwilling
to listen to the gospel of suffering which you must needs
learn? And thus Jesus brings in, though vaguely, the
argument from prophecy to sustain his new teaching of
the doctrine of the cross, and so returns to the central and
dominating theme of this section of the Gospel.

As this period of wandering in Gentile territory began
with the casting out of a demon from the daughter of the
Syrophœnician woman, so it now closes with a like mercy
to the tormented son of a father perplexed and distressed.

When Jesus and the three disciples who had been with
him came down to the foot of the Mount of Transfiguration, they found the other disciples sur-
rounded by a great crowd, in which were
scribes warmly disputing with the disciples.
When Jesus asked the meaning of the scene, a father in
the crowd told him that he had brought his afflicted
son to seek healing at his hands, and that, not finding
him, he had asked the disciples to cast the demon out

The Demoni-
ac Boy

108

of the boy; but, though they had tried, they could not do it. Some aspect of this failure was, therefore, the ground of the dispute with the scribes as well as of the peculiar excitement of the scene.

Jesus, hearing this explanation, rebuked that "faithless generation" and commanded the father to bring the boy to him. When this was done the demon threw the boy into a violent convulsion at the very feet of Jesus, so that all saw the completeness and malignity of its power. Jesus then elicited from the father the information that this condition had obtained from the very childhood of his son, so that all might know the long standing of the lad's affliction. These two factors, coupled with the disciples' inability to effect a cure, are designed to emphasize the difficulty of the case and the apparent hopelessness of any relief, and therefore to set off in the clearest terms the incomparable worth and power of faith.

For the demonstration of the power of faith is the central element in the incident. And so when the father pitifully turns to Jesus with the almost hopeless words, **Have Faith** "If thou canst do anything, have compassion on us and help us," Jesus reproves him for the faithlessness of "If thou canst," and assures him that "All things are possible to him that believeth." So long as the doubting attitude, "If thou canst," prevails, the power of Jesus, though ready, indeed, and sufficient, cannot be brought into effective action. The first step to relief must be the removal of the doubt that relief is possible. The father catches this idea; and he responds, feebly, but with intensest earnestness, "I believe; help thou mine unbelief."

When this barrier of unbelief is thus broken, and the crowd, especially curious to see what Jesus will do, keeps pressing together upon them, Jesus commands the demon to leave the boy and to trouble him no more. And with a last violent convulsion of his victim, the demon obeys; and the lad, released from its control, lies as one dead. But Jesus took him by the hand and raised him, and he stood up.

And thus, abruptly, the story of the healing ends; but not yet the incident. There remained the question of the failure of the disciples to effect the cure. In the light of their call "to have authority to cast out demons" (Mark 3: 15), and their success in so doing in their earlier mission (Mark 6: 13), and perhaps goaded by the gibes of the scribes (Mark 9: 14), they were sensitive and perplexed at their present impotence. And so, when they had come into a house, they asked of Jesus the explanation of their failure: "How is it that *we* [emphatic] could not cast it out?" "For the lack of sufficient prayer,"

Prayer

says Jesus in reply—meaning, doubtless, that same attitude which he describes in the parallel in Matthew (17: 20) when he says, "Because of your little faith," for the impotent disciples are included in that "faithless generation" which Jesus had before bemoaned and reproved.

And so this last miracle of the wandering—a miracle of the limitless power of faith—serves also, and sadly, to set off the disciples from their Master. They are not yet able to do his work; they are not yet thinking, with him, fully in the terms of God. And their failure here is in keeping with, and reflects, their attitude to his high, hard doctrine of the cross. How, then, shall they go on with

110

him, in understanding and sympathy, toward the tragic realization of that doctrine? If they are still lacking in prayerfulness and faith, surely they are but ill-prepared to share their Master's mind in the matter of his suffering or to walk with him his *via dolorosa*. They may go with him, indeed, to Jerusalem; but they will not go with his spirit or with his resources to meet the crisis that awaits them there. "For the lack of prayer"—sad words, and ominous.

111

CHAPTER VII

SETTING OUT TOWARD JERUSALEM

THE DOCTRINE OF THE CROSS (CONTINUED)

Mark 9: 30—10: 31

JESUS, as we have seen, has determined to go to Jerusalem in a last supreme effort to redeem the lost sheep of the house of Israel. He has elicited from his disciples, and has accepted and confirmed, their confession of his Messiahship. It is, therefore, a distinctly Messianic party, setting out upon a definite Messianic enterprise, that now leaves the vicinity of Mount Hermon, after the healing of the demoniac boy, and turns its steps toward Jerusalem.

As the Messiah

But the Leader of that party and his friends have very different ideas of the nature and issue of the enterprise upon which they are engaged. To Jesus, it was, for himself and, in a sense, for his followers, the Way of the Cross—a finding one's life in the kingdom of God by losing one's life in this world. But such a conception, though he had already tried to give it them, was still unacceptable to his friends. To them, as yet, the Messianic enterprise could by no means find its ultimate success through the death of the Messiah. A dead Messiah was a contradiction in terms, and death for Jesus would only prove that they had been in error in their identification of him as the Messiah. Their Messiah *must* triumph, and that without death; and this Messianic enterprise, because it was Messianic, *must* issue in the national deliverance and the establishment of Messiah upon the more glorious throne of David. The cross was still their stumblingblock; and

Jesus vs. the Disciples

they still needed much instruction to bring them to the mind of Jesus.

With this unsolved problem in their minds the little company left the vicinity of Hermon and passed through northeastern Galilee in secret; for Jesus **Secrecy** "would not that any man should know it." One of the reasons for this secrecy was doubtless the fact that they now reëntered the territory of Herod Antipas, with its unabated danger from the Court and the Pharisees—a danger that would certainly be enhanced, whether from the enthusiasm of the populace or from the fear and aggravated hostility of the upper classes, if it should become known that Jesus was specifically recognized as the Messiah and that he and his friends were setting forth upon a Messianic enterprise. But Mark does not even mention this reason. The only reason that he actually assigns for this desire for secrecy is that Jesus was teaching his disciples the doctrine of the cross. So fundamental, and now so urgent, was their instruction in this doctrine that Jesus did not want his teaching to be disturbed by any outside contacts or activities. He was primarily concerned with the preparation of his friends for the crisis that was before them all. But though he sought, indeed, to lighten the gloom of his forecast by the promise of his resurrection, "they understood not the saying, and were afraid to ask him."

But it was not merely the saying about the resurrection that "they understood not"; it was this whole doctrine of the cross, as it applied to their Master, and **Need of Instruction** as, in turn, it applied to themselves. For him, it meant rejection and death, and a resurrection to reverse these issues and vindicate his

8   **113**

place and claim; but if they did not understand the resurrection, they could not see beyond the rejection and the death, and consequently could find no place for them. And for them, in their turn and place, the doctrine of the cross meant, as Jesus had already indicated, a like spirit of generous self-forgetfulness and self-sacrifice. But they were no more ready to accept that doctrine for themselves than for their Master.

That fact was made evident by the matter of their discussion among themselves as they passed through Galilee to Capernaum; for they had been engaged in a dispute as to their relative greatness, probably having in view that Messianic kingdom which they supposed they were now on the way to Jerusalem to establish. (See another phase of this dispute in Mark 10: 35–45.) Such an attitude of narrow selfishness and egotism, involving, as it must, the corresponding discounting of others for the magnifying of one's self, was far from that willingness to take up the cross and follow Jesus which he had said was a condition of all true discipleship. If his cause was to be intrusted to these men, that attitude must be corrected, for it was centrally fatal to all that Jesus taught and lived for and was now about to die for.

Consequently, when they reached Capernaum, and had entered into a house—not further described, but probably not Peter's—Jesus took their dispute on the road as a starting point for instruction in the gospel of the cross in its application to them and to all his disciples. This teaching begins with the declaration of the primacy of humble, unselfish, and comprehensive helpfulness: "If any man would be first, he shall be last of all, and servant of all"; and it closes

True Greatness

114

with the counsel of acute and searching self-criticism, coupled with a tolerant and generous peace within the brotherhood: "Have salt in yourselves, and be at peace one with another."

For the greatness of place, with its necessary pride and exclusiveness, Jesus substitutes the greatness of an all-embracing service—not a sycophantic service to the great and the powerful who might give reward in earthly kind, but a service to the little and the weak, a service whose motive is love and whose rewards are the ineffable enrichment of the spirit of him who serves. And he illustrates this lesson by taking a little child of the house in his arms and telling them that the generous attitude that receives such a little one—obscure, helpless, needing love and care—in his name, will find its reward in the reception, along with the little one, of himself, yea, even of the Father who sent him.

Then says John, the son of Zebedee, in the only word from his lips alone that the Gospels have preserved: "We saw one casting out demons in thy name; and we forbade him, because he followed not us." The disciples' dispute about greatness had been limited to the comparative greatness of the members of their own circle, and perhaps one of their bases of comparison had been their respective success in the casting out of demons. Such a basis would be impaired, of course, if any one outside of that circle should be allowed to do the same thing. In any case, this stranger's act was an assumption of their prerogatives, which could not be tolerated. But Jesus rebuked their narrow exclusiveness, reminding them that the stranger was doing a good work, and doing it, too, in his name, and

John's
Lesson

therefore would scarcely be able to speak evil of him.
"For he that is not against us is for us." And even such
a little manifestation of sympathy as the gift of a cup of
cold water to his followers, because they are his followers,
shall not be forgotten or unrewarded.

This is the positive side of the generous and helpful attitude; but the negative side is no less important. Not to
hurt is the obverse of to help. And so Jesus warns them
not to cause the very least believer to stumble in faith
and life; it were better to be put to death. "And, in your
own case, whatever causes you to stumble must be
rigorously put away from you; for there is nothing in this
life comparable in value with the life to come, and he who
would win this higher life must resolutely repudiate anything that would defeat its attainment. You Twelve are
no exception to the rule of being made perfect through
suffering and self-denial, for every one shall be salted with
this fire, as, under the Law, every sacrifice, to be acceptable to God, must be sprinkled with salt (Lev. 2: 13).
This salt of suffering and self-denial, indeed, is good;
but it may lose its worth, its ends be defeated, if it be
viewed as good for others and not for our-
Take to Yourselves selves, helpful for them but not for us. And
you Twelve, with your mutual criticisms and
your disputes, your bigness and your littleness, must have
this salt in your several selves; criticize yourselves,
not your fellows; humble yourselves, not them; deny
yourselves, rather than demand self-denial on the part
of others in your behalf; and thus 'be at peace one with
another.'"

After this searching lesson, Jesus and the disciples left
Capernaum, and, probably by way of the southern shore

The Route of the Sea of Galilee, passed out of Galilee for the last time and crossed into the territory on the eastern side of the Jordan, through the Decapolis. This territory, which in some texts of Mark is called "Judæa beyond the Jordan," but is more commonly known as Peræa, extended, with somewhat indefinite outlines, down the eastern shore of the Jordan from the southern border of the Decapolis to the Dead Sea (and beyond), and contained the only considerable body of Palestinian Jews, outside of Judæa proper, that Jesus had not yet touched. This fact may have influenced his choice of route, though the shorter way down the west bank of the river through Samaria had its own peculiar difficulties, and Jewish travelers from Galilee to Jerusalem usually took this Perean route. The territory was coupled with Galilee to constitute the tetrarchy of Herod Antipas, and its main road was the highway of travel for religious leaders passing to and fro between Judæa and Galilee. It was, therefore, about as dangerous ground for Jesus as was Galilee itself.

But Jesus' movements were no longer secret. Probably there were many travelers already on the road making their way to Jerusalem for the approaching Feast of the Passover, and their presence would afford him both a field for work and a certain degree of popular protection. In any case, he has now come out of his retirement definitely to resume his work among and for the masses of his people; and so, as he journeyed through Peræa, "multitudes come together unto him again; and, as he was wont, he taught them again."

And there came, also, Pharisees! Just as they had met him on his former public return to Galilee with their de-

Divorce

mand for a sign from heaven, so now they meet him again when he reappears in the territory of Antipas. And the question that they propound to him is a peculiarly ominous one. "Is it lawful for a man to put away his wife?" they ask, trying him. Herod Antipas had done just that very thing: and his divorce was lawful (Deut. 24: 1). The Pharisees knew that, and they knew that Jesus knew it. They probably expected him, therefore, to answer this first question in the affirmative. But there was another aspect of Herod's behavior that was specifically contrary to the law: his marriage with his brother Philip's wife while Philip was yet living (Lev. 18: 16; 20: 21). To this, probably, the Pharisees proposed to advance, if Jesus gave affirmative answer to their first question. And it was for reproving Herod for the violation of this law that John the Baptist had but lately been put to death. If, now, Jesus accepted the Law of Deuteronomy, and so escaped their first attack, he would be equally certain to accept the Law of Leviticus and thus fall victim to their second attack, and render himself liable, now that he was in Herod's territory, to the same fate that had befallen John for the same cause.

One can scarcely pass this by without observing that these same Pharisees, sturdy champions of the Law that they were, were themselves able somehow to avoid this dilemma, and even to make common cause with the Herodians in the effort to put Jesus to death.

But if Jesus answered their first question in the negative, he would immediately run counter to the specific permission of the Law, and, at the same time, would appear as a critic of Herod's divorce, lawful though that was.

And thus both the Pharisees and the Herodians would have joint cause for further attack upon him.

Yet Jesus did answer, "No." He recognized the Law's permission of divorce, if the wife were given a written certificate of divorcement. That, indeed, had

No!

been an advance upon the previous perfect freedom of the husband to put away his wife without any consideration whatever for her feelings or her future. Even to have to give a certificate of divorce was some recognition of the dignity and rights of the wife; for its possession would at least indicate that she had been a lawful wife, and that, thus formally divorced, she was at liberty to contract another lawful marriage. But is this enough, the final word? On the contrary Jesus says, "For your hardness of heart he wrote you this commandment." It is neither adequate nor final; it is a concession to human stupidity and weakness, and is not in accordance with the divine will. That will may be seen in the account of the creation of man and woman (see Gen. 1: 27; 2: 24). There it will be seen that the relation of husband and wife is to be even closer and more tender than the relation of a man to his parents; that, indeed, "they are no more two, but one flesh," so that divorce is the hacking in two of a new and divinely approved unity. (And he adds, in private explanation to the disciples, that the remarriage of divorced persons is simply adultery, whereby he censures both Herod and Herodias.) "What therefore God hath joined together, let not man put asunder."

Here, then, Jesus specifically characterizes a law of Moses as defective, because of a "hardness of heart"

119

that would have no better, and sets over against it, and in place of it, a higher principle. He moves along the same line as in his former controversy with them (Mark 7: 1–23); and it is hard to say whether his characterization of the Mosaic Law or his statement of the reason for its deficiency would give the more offense. Certainly his statement would offend the Pharisees from one angle, and the Herodians from another; and while our narrative leaves the matter here abruptly, the situation is a factor in the controversy of Jesus with these two groups, and played its part in the issue of that controversy.

A Defective Law of Moses

This intrusion of the Pharisees broke with dramatic suddenness into Jesus' friendly intercourse with the multitudes. When it is past, and Jesus and the disciples have resumed their journey, two incidents occur that both illustrate the esteem in which Jesus was held and serve for the further instruction of the disciples along the lines of his last private teaching in Capernaum—the application of the gospel of the cross in generosity of attitude, sympathy, and self-denial.

(a) Certain fathers were bringing their children to Jesus that he might touch them. They felt that some virtue would be imparted even by the touch of so great and holy a man; and they felt, too, that he would be willing to receive and bless their little ones. But they had not counted on the disciples, and these now interposed between them and Jesus. What had Jesus to do with a lot of little children? He was engaged upon a great Messianic enterprise, and must not be disturbed with trifles. But Jesus, who may be said to have discovered children, was indignant at the callous-

The Children

120

ness and misunderstanding of his disciples, and commanded them to let the children come, because to such as they are—simple, direct, confiding, trustful, giving love to love and faith to faith—belongs the kingdom of God; and who should exclude from his presence these its natural representatives?[1] Indeed, childlikeness for all, in attitude toward and understanding of the great principles of the kingdom as Jesus set them forth and embodied them— for all, including you Twelve who think so loftily and so selfishly about the kingdom—is an absolute requisite for entering into it. And so he took the children in his arms and blessed them—a picture of his own tenderness and understanding, set against the dark background of the disciples' erroneous standards and ideals.

(b) Few things are more highly prized by men than wealth, and yet few things tend more subtly or more surely to deaden the sense of higher values. It is a
Wealth   menace to childlikeness; and it is disposed to interpret everything, even the kingdom of God, in its own terms, and to measure everything by its own values. It is often made a standard of greatness and then expects, and receives from those who mind the things of men, a sycophantic regard to which, on the basis of the things of God,

[1]Bacon says: "It is the humble position—not *dis*position—of a child which forms the point of comparison. Children are not more humble than other people, but what they receive comes to them of grace and not as earned, or by enforceable right." This, too, is true; but it is inadequate. For the sophisticated standards and artificial distinctions of maturity do not belong to childhood. They are, in large measure, if not wholly, acquired from one's elders. Who has not seen rich children and poor, high-placed and lowly, playing contentedly together, without any sense of incongruity or impropriety?

121

it is by no means entitled. All this is neither new nor rare. It was true in the days of Jesus, and, to a considerable extent, in the circle of his disciples. They had, indeed, "left all" to follow him; but in exact proportion as they expected that following to lead them into a material kingdom, they had not passed from a lower area of thinking and of values into a higher, but had merely left the little in order to gain the much.

And so, just as the incident of the children was used by Jesus to teach them childlikeness, the immediately following incident of a rich man's contact with him was used to teach them the related lesson of self-denial and otherworldliness, to lift them to a higher level of thinking in regard to material possessions.

As they continued their journey toward Jerusalem, a rich man came running to Jesus—a rich man with a sense of need and a hope that Jesus can satisfy his heart's desire. He wants eternal life; but he has no assurance that it is, or will be, his. He seems to have done all that the Law required, and yet he is conscious that something still is lacking. Has he perchance overlooked or omitted anything in the way of the Law? for he could scarcely think of any other way to find his place in the world to come. He knows of Jesus as a remarkable and eminent teacher; perhaps he can help him in his perplexity.

His salutation is respectful, and his question reflects his legalistic training and ideas. "Good Master," he says—a salutation that Jesus repudiates, as indicating some levity or misconception of the nature and center of "goodness"—"what *shall I do* that I may inherit eternal life?" For the way of *doing* was the scribal way. And on this basis

"What Shall I Do?"

122

Jesus first cites the inquirer to the essential commandments on right relations to one's fellows. But these, says the rich man, I have kept from my youth, probably meaning from his twelfth year, when he had become a son of the Law and personally responsible for its observance.

Jesus, it will be noted, has quite ignored all trivial traditions and mere transient or ceremonial commandments. The things that he has touched are things that he himself approved and taught: they are matters of abiding validity and worth. And so, accepting the rich man's statement as literally true, "Jesus, looking upon him, loved him." The man was, so far as he had gone, a proper object of his approval. Certainly no one could hope for eternal life who ignored such principles as are expressed in these commandments.

And yet the man's sense of need was well grounded, and what he needed was, in effect, just that message of the cross that Jesus was trying to impart to his disciples. He was leaning, perhaps more heavily than he realized, upon the things of this world; and, in just that proportion, undervaluing the things of that world to come in which he sought eternal life. He needed recentralization, new motives, values, loyalties.

And so Jesus told him first that he must part with his wealth, part with it irretrievably by distributing it to the poor; and promised him that, in place
The Answer of these earthly treasures, and for their renunciation, he should have treasures in heaven, meaning, substantially, that eternal life which he was seeking. And then Jesus does the unusual thing of inviting this man, when he shall have renounced his earthly

123

treasures, to attach himself to his own person and become one of his personal followers. It was a call to apostleship on the basis of the doctrine of the cross.

But Jesus' remedy is too drastic; those heavenly treasures are too vague and far away; and so "he went away sorrowful, for he was one that had great possessions." His wealth had caused him to stumble; but he could not, or would not, cut it off.

Too Drastic

When the rich man was thus sadly gone, Jesus drew out a general lesson from the incident for the benefit of the disciples. Not in this man's case alone, but in many cases, worldly wealth is a cause of stumbling. It is no easy matter to enter the kingdom of God, and the difficulty is greatly enhanced by the possession of wealth. Indeed, "It is easier for a camel to go through a needle's eye, than for a rich man to enter the kingdom of God," a fine and pregnant hyperbole.

The disciples were amazed at such teaching. And small wonder; for it involved both a radical reëstimate of wealth, which is never easy, and a radical break with the scribal interpretation and program of religion. If, as the scribes taught, eternal life is to be attained by the exact observance of minute and multiplied "religious" requirements, as distinguished from the filial attitude toward God and fraternal relations with men, the rich would certainly have a better chance than the poor of attaining it, for they have both the time and the means more fully to meet those requirements. And, as a matter of fact, this scribal interpretation did close the door of hope to multitudes of the people, who had neither the time nor the money to con-

"Then Who Can Be Saved?"

form to the program prescribed. And so the disciples said, "If a rich man cannot be saved, who can?"

Jesus had just shown them how one rich man might have been saved. But, in his case, it was by first becoming poor. And this was no universal rule of thumb for attaining eternal life, as though the renunciation of property, in itself, as some *opus operatum*, insured the reception of heavenly treasures. That would, indeed, be to make Jesus an exponent of scribal theory; on a new basis, to be sure, but no less utterly repugnant to the very genius of his whole interpretation of religion. And the problem was not to save a *rich* man by first making him poor, but to save a rich *man*—just a man—though still rich.

And yet the incident just closed in sorrow would illustrate and enforce the universal principle. With men, indeed, says Jesus, thinking in common worldly terms and seeking salvation by methods in conformity with those terms, it is impossible for the rich to be saved. For salvation involves new terms. But the task is not impossible with God; for all things are possible with him. He can lead a rich man to a better way of thinking, where he will repudiate the primacy of his wealth, and will receive the kingdom of God, on its own conditions, even as a little child.

Then Peter raised the question of the application of this incident and teaching to himself and his fellow disciples: "Lo, we have left all, and have followed thee."

"What About Us?" We are, therefore, entitled to treasures in heaven, as you promised the rich inquirer. (These treasures were "laid up in heaven," but to be bestowed and enjoyed on earth, when the new age should come in.) And apparently Peter means to imply that "*we*" are entitled to special consideration. But Jesus in his answer lays down a general principle that applies to the Twelve as well as to all others. Whoever, he says, has renounced any of the dear and precious things of this life, *for his sake*, shall certainly receive his reward. He will find that he receives, even in this present age, more, in the treasures of his new fellowship, than he has given up (though he must also look for persecutions); and in the coming age he will receive eternal life. But as for the assumed priority of the Twelve, "many that are first shall be last; and the last first." "Not the most forward claimant will be best off in the end" (Menzies), for the doctrine of the cross cannot be capitalized.

CHAPTER VIII

ARRIVAL AT JERUSALEM: THE TRIUMPHAL ENTRY

MARK 10: 32–11: 11

JESUS and his company now enter upon the last stage of their journey to Jerusalem. Jesus is walkng alone, in advance of the rest. Behind him come the apostles; and farther back (if we follow our common text) is an undefined group of other followers, perhaps composed of travelers toward Jerusalem who had loosely attached themselves to Jesus' company as he passed through Peræa.

Approaching the City

The disciples were filled with amazement, and these others with fear, as they thus followed Jesus. The disciples knew that they were engaged upon a Messianic mission, and possibly some idea of this sort was in the minds of these other followers of their Master. Such an approach to Jerusalem, so humble, so peaceful, so unlike the common expectations of Messiah's appearance, would, therefore, naturally arouse sentiments of amazement and anxiety in those who took part in it. What sort of Messiah could this be, and what hope could be placed in such a Messianic enterprise? What of the apocalyptic appearance, or of the militant leadership, of the Messiah?

And so now again, as upon their first open confession of his Messiahship, and as in their last secret passage through Galilee, Jesus undertakes to teach the disciples the doctrine of the cross, both in regard to himself and as it should apply to them. And the necessity for this teaching, as it might be inferred

Anticipation: Jesus

127

from the nearness of the event, is abundantly demonstrated by the attitude and behavior of the disciples themselves.

They and their Master were approaching their objective in very different minds. Jesus foresaw rejection, humiliation, death, but a vindicating resurrection, and a triumph to follow and to be attained through his sufferings, a ransoming of many by the way of his death. And he now sought again, by repeating his forecast of the immediate issue of their enterprise, to correct their mistaken anticipations and thus to prepare them for the shock of the actual event.

But the disciples, despite their present amazement at the form of their Messianic approach to the city, and despite Jesus' repeated efforts to bring them to his own mind, were thinking in terms of a Messianic kingdom, powerful and glorious, in whose establishment they were about to have a share. Peter's question, "What shall *we* have therefore?" (implied in Mark 10: 28 and specifically stated in the parallel in Matthew 19: 27), is in their minds. And their dispute on comparative greatness, already, but ineffectually, rebuked before they left Galilee (Mark 9: 33–37), reappears in urgent and concrete form as the time for the realization of their aspirations draws near.

The Disciples

By Jesus' own acts Peter and James and John had been constituted an inner circle of his most intimate and confidential friends, and they might, therefore, expect a like preëminence in the kingdom which he was about to establish. But James and John are brothers, and they want for themselves a preference even within this inner circle. They are not

James and John

128

disposed to give place to Peter, or the rest, nor yet to leave the whole matter entirely in the hands of Jesus. And, as the time is now so short, they must needs take some action to bring their claims to the attention of Jesus and to have their superior status definitely settled by him in advance. And so they approach Jesus with the general and vague request that he will do them a favor. But before he commits himself, Jesus wants to know what that favor is. And then they ask for themselves the two highest places of honor "in his glory," meaning, in that glorious Messianic kingdom which is soon to appear.

But Jesus sees the way to his glory through intervening suffering and death. And as he may not avoid that way, so neither may it be avoided by any who would share in the glory beyond. And so he asks James and John whether they are able to walk that way, seeing that this is the only way and they have not taken it into account in the making of their request. "Yes," they said, "we are able and prepared to pay any price for the boon we ask. We will share your sufferings, if only thereby we may attain our coveted preëminence in your glory." And thereby they give expression to a loyalty and devotion at once over-estimated and pledged in the expectation of a great and selfishly sought reward. They propose to carry the Petrine "*We* have left all" to its limit; but they expect to receive in return a proportionately abundant answer to the question, "What shall *we* have therefore?" Their attitude does not necessarily involve any appreciation of, or assent to, the idea of a suffering Messiah, but only that, if Jesus' gloomy forebodings (as they thought) should in fact be realized, they were nevertheless able and

9   129

willing to go through his experiences of suffering in order to obtain the honors they sought.

But honors in Jesus' kingdom thus selfishly sought, involving the exaltation of one's self with a corresponding depreciation of others, are not to be obtained even by the way of suffering. The doctrine of the cross thus capitalized loses its distinctive quality and becomes only another road to the gratification of personal ambition. Even to "give my body to be burned" will profit nothing when that apparent self-sacrifice is only another form of real self-seeking. Self-sacrifice must be made for others; it cannot be made for one's self.

And so Jesus tells these brothers that they shall, indeed, drink of his cup and be baptized with his baptism, meaning that they should suffer martyrdom as the penalty of their devotion to himself.

An Impossible Request

(How this was realized in the case of James we are told in Acts 12: 1; but concerning John's fate the Scriptures are silent, as they record the death of no apostle except James.) But, even so, he cannot grant their request; for "to sit on my right hand or on my left hand is not mine to give; but it is for them for whom it hath been prepared." Such a matter is in the hands of the Father only. Jesus himself cannot bestow the honors of the kingdom in response to mere request or as mere personal favors. The conditions of their attainment are fixed, and they will be bestowed on those for whom, under these conditions, they are prepared. "As if a just king were presiding over some athletic contest and some of his friends should come to him and say, 'Give us the crowns', he would say, 'It is not mine to give; but if any man shall contend and win, for him the crown has been

130

prepared,'" said Theophylact in explanation of these words. There can be no favoritism in the kingdom of God.

When the ten other apostles heard of this action of James and John, they were naturally indignant. But this was not because the brothers had such poor and unworthy ideas of the coming kingdom and greatness therein, for the group was at one in their ideas of these matters. It was because James and John had taken what the rest regarded as an unfair advantage over them in privately seeking for themselves the preference which they all desired. It was another phase, acute and personal, of their former dispute about greatness.

The scene must have been very distressing to Jesus, for nothing could more clearly indicate the deep divergence of their minds from his; and that, too, despite his previous instruction and upon the eve of the crisis for which he had been trying to prepare them. But with great patience and tenderness he undertook again to teach them the better way. "Your idea of greatness as lordship over others," he says, "belongs to the Gentile way of thinking."

Among them, those who seem to rule—for
True Greatness their rule is only "seeming," either because it is based upon unsound principles or because the apparent rulers are, in fact, only the puppets of the real demonic rulers whom they represent—lord it over others; and "the great" are those who exercise authority over their subordinates. Scarcely could even the most stupid and selfish disciple, being a Jew, miss the implication of this statement; for certainly the kingdom of God, even as they understood and expected it, could not be founded or administered upon the common principles of

131

the Gentiles. But Jesus makes the implication specific: "But it shall not be so among you." Your greatness is not to be seeming, but real: not representative of demonic powers and standards, but representative of that Messiah in whose kingdom it is to be attained. And as he "came not to be ministered unto, but to minister, and to give his life a ransom for many," so your coveted greatness is to be found in the most generous and unselfish service. Not service, indeed, that looks beyond itself to selfish reward, when the rule of service shall give place to the luxury of being served, but service as in itself great and worthful, and finding its rewards in its results in and for others: the giving one's life, if one may so say, a ransom for many, the price paid for their release from bondage and peril, meagerness and despair, and all the grim consequences of sin; to see of the travail of one's soul and therein to be satisfied.

The desire for greatness is not here reprehended; but the common standards of greatness are revolutionized. And, in this splendid conception, self-realization and the common good are fused in a novel and gracious unity. Whoso finds his greatness in service will make the larger contribution to the common good the greater he becomes; forgetting himself, he will find a realm in which, to his surprise, he will be remembered; losing his life, he will find it. Here is a new attitude, a new form of self-expression, which itself is greatness. Nothing from without can add to or diminish its intrinsic quality. No wonder, as Bacon says, that "it becomes to Paul the keystone of a new sociology of the entire creation of personal beings."

Jesus and his company now cross to the western side of the Jordan, out of Peræa into Judæa, and come to the

132

Jericho
ancient city of Jericho, some five miles from the river and about three times that distance from Jerusalem. And here Jesus, for the first time, publicly receives and accepts a Messianic salutation, a fitting introduction to his Messianic entrance into Judea.

As they were passing out of Jericho on the way to Jerusalem, a certain Bartimæus, a blind beggar, was sitting by the wayside. When he heard that it was Jesus who was passing in the throng, he began to cry aloud for help: "Thou son of David, have mercy on me!" And when he refused to be silenced by the rebukes of many, Jesus bade them summon him into his presence, and, in response to his request, restored his sight with a word, "Go thy way; thy faith hath made thee whole. And straightway he received his sight, and followed him in the way."

"Son of David"

But this incident is not related for the sake of the miracle, but because of the salutation, "Thou son of David," with which Bartimæus addressed Jesus. This was Messianic (Rom. 1: 3), and it strikes the first note in Jesus' Messianic welcome to Jerusalem. That such a salutation seemed premature, inappropriate on the lips of a blind beggar, dangerous, probably explains the efforts of the many to silence Bartimæus. But Jesus himself, altogether in contrast to his previous reticence, now makes no objection to such a greeting. The time for silence is past; his offer of himself as Messiah in Jerusalem is at hand. Bartimæus only gives voice to what the apostles already knew and what was doubtless in the minds of many others of the attendant crowd. He brings to a head and to expression many vague and unformed wonderings, providing the

The Messiah

133

answer to the old and widespread question, "Who, then, is this?" And thus unwittingly, but appropriately and opportunely, he introduces Jesus' Messianic approach to Jerusalem.

After the long, hard climb of a dozen miles from Jericho to the vicinity of Bethany, which, in turn, lay about two miles from Jerusalem, Jesus pauses to make provision for his formal and conspicuous entrance into the city. He is at the head of a crowd of enthusiastic followers; he has publicly accepted the title and rôle of the Messiah; but he will not enter Jerusalem weary, dusty, and unnoticed. On the contrary, since he now wants his Messianic mission known, he will enter the city in such stirring and impressive fashion as to command its attention and to center its interest in himself. But he will come in peace, and not as the common type of Messianic agitator with his program of military violence and political revolution.

The Triumphal Entry

And so he sends two of his disciples into the village, Bethany or Bethphage, and tells them that they will there find a young colt that has never yet been ridden and that, with proper explanation to its owner, they are to bring the animal back to him. When they had done this, and some had thrown their outer garments as saddlecloths upon the animal, Jesus mounted it and the company resumed its way, with Jesus now riding in its midst. And as they advanced the Messianic enthusiasm of the crowd broke forth unchecked. Some spread their garments in the road, while others cast thereon leaves and branches brought from adjacent fields, to carpet Messiah's way, and those that went before him and those that followed shouted in snatches of Psalms, "Save now! Blessed is

134

he that cometh in the name of the Lord! Blessed is the
kingdom that cometh, the kingdom of our father David!"
And thus Jesus, as the Messiah, came into Jerusalem with
a popular welcome that is the climax of his favor with the
common people.

This triumphal entry is the first scene in the climax of
Jesus' appeal to the nation in behalf of the rule of God.
For, in addition to its religious (or cultus)
centrality, all that remained to the Jews of
national independence and authority centered
in Jerusalem and the temple. An appeal to
the nation, as a nation, must be made there. Without
such appeal Jesus' mission would have been incomplete.
He would have been a provincial, a Galilean, prophet;
and the seat of the nation's life and ills would have been
untouched. No sort of general repentance or reform could
have been brought about, the kingdom of God could not
come to the Jewish nation, while conditions in Jerusalem
remained unchanged. The leadership of the nation must
be brought to repentance, displaced, or destroyed before
"the lost sheep of the house of Israel" could find their
proper folding and the rule of God could come. Jerusalem
must be challenged to choose between Jesus and the Sanhedrin, whether Pharisees or Sadducees; and the triumphal entry was the beginning of this challenge.

But, as Jesus clearly saw, the movement was as dangerous as it was imperative. Besides the Pharisees and
Herodians, there were two other groups of
leaders that he must encounter in Judæa and
Jerusalem that had played little or no part in
the remoter and obscurer field of Galilee. These were:

(a) The Sadducees, heading up in the priestly hierocracy

135

that controlled the temple and the worship that centered therein. They had not appeared in Galilee;
The Sadducees but Jerusalem was the seat and center of their authority. And, however much they might differ from the Pharisees on other matters, it was a foregone conclusion that they would be at one with them in their hostility to Jesus and his mission, especially if that mission took on a Messianic aspect that threatened either the political *status quo* or the religious position, perquisites, and authority of the Sadducaic party.

(b) The Roman authority, whose local head was the procurator, Pontius Pilate. This authority was not **Romans** directly exercised in Galilee. Herod Antipas, as tetrarch, with a certain quasi-independence, stood between it and the common people. But Jesus' activity had there encountered the suspicion and hostility of the Herodians because of its Messianic complexion; and in Judæa the Roman authority was apt to be no less suspicious and was more powerful and terrible. For while the Romans were very tolerant of the practices and parties of recognized religions in the empire, they were acutely suspicious of anything that threatened the public peace or savored of insurrection, and repressed any such movement with unsparing and dreadful severity.

Jesus' entrance into Jerusalem had, indeed, been planned and carried through at a time and in a manner as nearly as possible to avoid the suspicion of political purpose or insurrectionary agitation; and the Roman authorities took no notice of it. Probably they regarded it as a not unusual outburst of religious enthusiasm on the part of a band of pilgrims coming up to the Feast of the Passover. Nevertheless, any Messianic enterprise, how-

136

ever politically inoffensive, would have to take account of the common Roman attitude and would not find it easy to justify itself to Rome's acute and suspicious judgment.

And besides all this, the crowds that escorted Jesus into the city were thinking in terms of imminent national deliverance, of the coming kingdom of their
People father David. Whatever were his Messianic ideas and purposes, theirs (if known) would certainly not seem innocuous to their Roman masters. Consequently, the very Messianic popularity that Jesus now sought was full of danger because of the Messianic ideas of the crowds with which, for the time, that popularity was attained. If Jesus were their sort of Messiah, he might very easily now start an armed insurrection; but if he were not their sort, he might expect them promptly to turn against him, and with the more bitterness because of their disappointment; unless, indeed, he could bring them to his mind and to the acceptance of himself as the sort of Messiah that he was and proposed to be.

And herein lies the explanation of his present course. This popular recognition of his Messiahship, full of difficulty and danger as it was, was necessary to
His Purpose the accomplishment of his purpose. He was not entering the city as a political revolutionist. He had no designs of violence against the Roman Empire. But he did come as a religious revolutionist, the champion of the lost sheep of the house of Israel. It was his purpose to win for them their place in the covenant of sonship from which the Pharisees and the Sadducees had in effect excluded them. He wanted to change or to destroy the perverse religious leadership of these blind leaders of the blind so that the unchurched and un-

privileged masses might enter into their precious religious heritage, and become, in simplicity and truth, the children of the Great King. In a word, he wanted to make Jerusalem, the center of the nation's life, fit to be the center of the kingdom of God. And that required either the conversion of the Sanhedrin or the national repudiation of its leadership and control.

Sadly enough, he could expect little or nothing from the Pharisees and the Sadducees except increasing opposition to a program that would certainly A New Loyalty destroy their influence and leadership. But he invited the people to another shepherding, to take his yoke upon them, to learn of him, and so to find rest for their souls. Not by violence either against Rome or against the Sanhedrin, but by a better understanding and a peaceful change of estimates and of loyalties, he would bring the nation to the knowledge and the joy of God.

But this must evidently be done through popular recognition and support. He could save the people only if the people would accept him as their Saviour. The Use of Popularity And so, despite the dangers both from those in power and from the misunderstandings of the people, Jesus chose to offer himself to Jerusalem in the midst of the shouting throngs to whose religious deliverance his life was dedicated.

After thus entering the city, Jesus went into the temple and looked around upon what was going on there; and then, since it was now evening, went out to Jesus Visits the Temple Bethany with the Twelve to spend the night. And what he had seen in the temple lay heavy upon him.

138

CHAPTER IX

THE CONFLICT IN THE TEMPLE

MARK 11: 12–12: 44

WHAT Jesus had seen in the temple filled him with the deepest indignation. The Court of the Gentiles had been

Temple Profaned

turned into an Eastern bazaar, operated for the profit of the higher Sadducæan priesthood. It was filled with traders, trafficking, indeed, in "religious" merchandise—the required sacrifices, and the sacred shekel for the temple tax—but, nevertheless, at the best, disquieting, irreverent, and unseemly, and depriving the Gentiles of the use of the only part of the temple that had been set aside for them. And, to add to the noise and confusion, men with burdens in their arms or on their shoulders were using the Court as a common thoroughfare, a short-cut to their destination, in place of circling the temple walls. Besides all this, the traffic was carried on for private profit, and the grossest extortion was practiced upon those who needed and must have its merchandise for the discharge of the religious obligations laid upon them by the Law. "What had once been 'a house of prayer' for all the people had become a veritable 'den of robbers.' The extortion practiced by the priesthood under the guise of Mosaic requirement is something well-nigh incredible. And under the unscrupulous 'hissing brood of Annas' it was carried to lengths hitherto unheard-of. The requirement of priestly inspection of sacrificial victims gave opportunity for an odious monopoly. Annas himself maintained a 'Bazaar of Doves,' where priests controlled the sale of

139

this offering, prescribed in the law as *that of the poor*. Even the lower orders of the priesthood were shamelessly mulcted, while assassination and intrigue marked the lives of a high-priestly caste, whose very name of 'Sadducee' became a synonym for blank irreligion (Acts 23:8)." (Bacon.)

Something of this Jesus had seen when he went into the temple and looked around on the first afternoon of his arrival in Jerusalem, before he withdrew to Bethany to spend the night. And that scene was in his mind when he set out from Bethany to return to the city on the following morning, as is indicated by the parabolic miracle with which the day began.

His Father had planted an orchard of figs, the nations of the earth. One tree had been the object of his special care, his Chosen People of Israel. The time for figs was not yet for the general orchard, but ought to be for this particular tree. The gardeners had, indeed, brought the tree to abundant leafage, which ought to assure the presence of fruit. But the hungry man, coming to that tree for the fruit that it promised, would be deceived; for he would find no fruit thereon, nothing but the leaves that had deceived and disappointed him. Such a tree could only be accursed and destroyed.

The
Fig Tree

Something like this is the meaning of the cursing of the fig tree. But it is probable that Jesus had in mind at this stage, not the destruction of the people of Israel as God's chosen people, but the destruction of that perverse system of religious leadership which had brought about this abundant leafage of religiosity with its tragic absence of the real fruits of

The
Leaders

140

religion. He is contemplating the leadership of the Pharisees and the Sadducees, against which his whole life has been a protest, and for the overthrow of which and the inauguration of a better day he is now offering himself to Jerusalem as the Messiah of God. The curse and the consequent destruction may have to be more comprehensive, as soon proved to be the case; but only if this leadership cannot be otherwise destroyed, and the people cannot be persuaded to accept in its place Jesus—as he was, not as they would have him be—as the Messiah whom God had sent for their deliverance.

At the moment the people were enthusiastic for Jesus; but he knew too well the erroneous basis of that enthusiasm, and that there was little or no chance of its accepting that profound reinterpretation that would bring it into conformity to his own purpose and work. He must take one step at a time; and his present popularity, however mistaken in its basis, is a background and a protection for his first attack upon the religious leadership of the Sadducees and the Pharisees.

And so, when he and the disciples came to Jerusalem and entered into the temple, Jesus cast out of the Court of the Gentiles those who were occupying it **The Temple Cleansed** with their traffic and defiling it with their frauds, and stopped its use as a common passageway for the hurrying bearers of burdens; and he justified and interpreted his act to the amazed spectators by citations from the prophets. Had not Isaiah said, "My house shall be called a house of prayer (and that, too) for all the nations"? But this gracious purpose of the temple is debased and defeated by what is going on here. How can this be a house of prayer for any

141

one, and especially for the nations, when it is filled with the clamor of the market place, and the Court of the Nations has become a common bazaar? (It is certainly too narrow a view of Jesus to suppose that, though his own personal mission was specifically to the lost sheep of the house of Israel, he took no interest in the Gentiles and found no ground of offense in the fact that they were deprived of the privileges of worship graciously provided for them in the very structure and arrangement of the temple itself. His view was certainly not less generous than the views of other and older prophets of his people.) And had not Jeremiah characterized this house of prayer as "a den of robbers"? And the people themselves who were robbed by these traffickers had the amplest evidence that Jeremiah's words fitly described the situation of which they were the victims. Certainly, then, when Messiah should come suddenly to his temple, his first task would be to cleanse its sacred precincts of this deep-seated and deadly abuse. And so this act of Jesus was the natural sequel of his Messianic entrance into the city, as it was the first scene in his final and fatal controversy with the religious leaders, whose power and whose system must be broken up to make way for the coming Rule of God.

The leaders thus attacked showed no inclination to come to terms with their attacker. Indeed, both they and Jesus perceived that no sort of compromise was possible. They represented irreconcilable attitudes, and the one or the other must be destroyed in the conflict that Jesus had precipitated. And the lust for power and the lust for money made common cause with the misinterpretation of religion to do away with Jesus; for the leaders of the priestly party

Jesus Must Be Destroyed

142

of the Sadducees and the scribes of the Pharisees, when they heard of Jesus' act and his teaching in the temple, "sought how they might destroy him." For "they feared him" because of his popularity with the people. But just as that popularity increased his menace to themselves, so it served, for the time, to protect Jesus from their vengeance, and they dared not lay hold upon him openly in the presence of the people. They must either wean the people from him or destroy him with more or less of secrecy. But, however it must be accomplished, their minds were made up to compass his destruction.

Jesus would not give them any unnecessary opportunity to assassinate him or to arrest him privately. He would be safer outside of the walls of the city; and so, as his custom was ("whenever evening came"), at the close of the day he withdrew to spend the night with friends in Bethany or in the open air upon the Mount of Olives.

Jesus Withdraws at Night

On the following morning, as Jesus and the disciples were returning to Jerusalem, Peter said to him, "The fig tree which thou cursedst is withered away," and Jesus took the occasion to teach him and the other disciples a lesson in the power of faith and prayer and in the need for the forgiving spirit. In view of the struggle on which they had entered the disciples needed, and would increasingly need, to learn this lesson, if they would meet it and its issues in the mind of their Master. For the lesson reflects his mind as he faced the situation.

A Needed Lesson

The ultimate issue of the controversy was certain. Jesus had no doubt whatever that the leadership and system that so grossly misrepresented God and misled

143

the people would be broken up and destroyed in favor of that truth which it was his mission to represent and declare. But the victory was not yet won, and no easy optimism at initial success blinded him to the difficulties and dangers of his task. The thought of victory through death, with which he had set his face steadfastly toward Jerusalem, was not expunged from his mind by the popular enthusiasm of his reception or the success of his first encounter with the leaders of the people. Nevertheless, whatever the time or the means, his faith in the power of the God for whom he spoke and was prepared to die was inviolate and inviolable; and he would impart of that faith, with its patience, to his disciples.

Jesus' Own Attitude

Jesus' understanding of the situation was immediately vindicated by the event. For when he and the disciples reached Jerusalem and entered the temple, a delegation from the Sanhedrin, "the chief priests, and the scribes, and the elders," came to him as he was walking therein and demanded his credentials. This they had a right and were, indeed, obligated to do, if the temple was not to become the prey of every wandering enthusiast; and thus their challenge brought Jesus face to face with the highest constituted authorities of his people, in the due exercise of their recognized rights, and therefore with all the presumptions of order in their favor. That the challenge was not friendly is not surprising, and does not impair its legitimacy. In due and proper form it raised the crucial question of Jesus' presence and mission in Jerusalem.

Jesus Challenged

"By what (sort of) authority doest thou these things? and who gave thee this authority?" they demanded.

144

His
Authority

"By what sort of authority" is explained by the phrase in Jesus' answer, "from heaven, or from men." His questioners wanted to know whether he claimed to have human or divine authority for his actions; whether he was a popular agitator, the head of a popular protest, relying upon the support of the crowds that followed him, or whether he came as a prophet, or even as the Messiah, and so claimed sanction and authority from God. What they really wanted was to elicit from Jesus an affirmation or a denial of his Messiahship, which, as they doubtless now knew, had been openly asserted in the Triumphal Entry and was implied in his purging of the temple.

Jesus' answer falls into two parts. He asks his questioners first to explain what they mean by different sorts

His Reply

of authority; but, to make their definition clear and pertinent, he confines it to a single and conspicuous case. "Let me ask you a single question; and when you answer that, I will answer you. What sort of authority was behind the ministry of John the Baptist, was his baptism from heaven, or from men?" Jesus himself had received that baptism; and many doubtless, besides his personal disciples, regarded him as the Baptist's greater successor, the continuer and perfecter of his work, the Coming One for whom John's Great Repentance was to prepare the way. He might now, therefore, either (a) claim the Baptist's authority for his course, or (b) assert the possession of a similar divine authority, which the people had recognized but these leaders had ignored in the case of John. In either case, a definition of the Baptist would make possible and defend a definition of himself. And just as Jesus was coupled in popular thought

10   145

with the Baptist, so the attitude of his questioners toward him would be coupled with their remembered attitude toward his forerunner.

They were, therefore, now in a dilemma. If Jesus proposed to attach himself and his ministry in any way to John, their attitude toward him would involve their attitude toward John. But they could not acknowledge that John's authority was from heaven without convicting themselves, because they had refused to receive him; and they could not openly say that John's authority was only from men without danger of violence at the hands of the people, "for all verily held John to be a prophet." Since they were thus in no position to define the different sorts of authority, had, indeed, shown themselves unable to recognize that sort that was from heaven in the case of John, they could give no answer to Jesus' question. And so he, for his part, having embarrassed his questioners by the very mention of John, bringing to remembrance their attitude toward him and the cleavage between them and the people in regard to him, refused to answer a question whose basis they would not define, and concerning which, in John's case, they had shown themselves such incompetent judges.

But while Jesus thus refused to give any specific answer to the question of the delegation from the Sanhedrin, his very mention of John had been suggestive of his Messianic claims; and he now proceeds, in the second part of his answer, to develop that suggestion in the veiled form of the Parable of the Vineyard, adapted from Isaiah 5: 1–7. A certain man, said he, had planted a vineyard; and, having made all necessary

The Questioners Silenced — marginal note

The Vineyard — marginal note

146

preparations for expected returns therefrom, had let it out to husbandmen for cultivation during his absence. From time to time, as the seasons came around, the owner had sent his servants to collect from the renters his share of the fruits of the vineyard. But the renters had treated these servants with contempt and violence, and had consistently refused to make any returns to the owner of the vineyard. At last the owner decided to send his son, seeing that he could get no returns through other messengers; for he said to himself, "They will reverence my son." But the husbandmen's attitude toward the servants was only intensified by the appearance of the son, for they saw in him the heir, and supposed that by murdering him they could get possession of the property. And so they killed the son, and cast his dead body out of the vineyard. But this last act of ingratitude, dishonesty, and disrespect finally broke the owner's patience and aroused his wrath. "What therefore will the lord of the vineyard do? he will come and destroy the husbandmen, and will give the vineyard unto others."[1]

This is Jesus' real answer to the question of the authorities. Though it is veiled in parabolic form for safety's sake, safety from them and safety from the wild enthusiasm of the people which an open declaration of Messiahship would arouse, they could not fail to see its application to themselves and to

The "Son"

---

[1] The added quotation from Psalm 118 (22, 23) changes the figure and contemplates another issue. In it, the rulers are builders who reject a certain stone (Jesus), which later, by God's act, is made the chief corner stone of another and better building. This contemplates the high destiny of Jesus; but the parable contemplates the destiny of the husbandmen and of the vineyard which had been intrusted to their care.

Jesus. They are the renters of the vineyard and Jesus is the son of the owner, demanding of them his dues. He does, therefore, claim to be the Messiah (in his own sense); his mission is a Messianic one. He knows, too, of their implacable hostility, their purpose to put him to death. And he warns them that through the very accomplishment of that purpose they will bring about their own destruction and the transference of the vineyard to other and more worthy representatives of its owner, though he does not say who these representatives are to be.

It was this penetrating description of themselves that most impressed, and most incensed, these questioners of Jesus. Their attitude toward him was exposed as the traditional attitude of their class to God's earlier messengers. (Compare Stephen's speech in the seventh chapter of Acts.) They had never been disposed to recognize the divine authority of the prophets; and now they were even less disposed to recognize his authority, though he was the Beloved Son. But God's judgment was now upon them, and they should be divested of the power and privileges which they had so long abused. And so, in their anger, "they sought to lay hold on him; for they perceived that he spake the parable against them." They dared not act openly for fear of the people, and so they left him and went away. But not with any idea of giving up the contest. On the contrary, the more clearly they saw that one side or the other must be destroyed in the struggle, the more determined were they that Jesus should be the one destroyed. If they could not take him openly because of the support of the people, they might either make such a breach between him and his followers

148

as would leave him at their mercy, or they might find some way to take him secretly, separated from his supporters.

They ultimately succeeded by the latter method, as the later narrative shows; but, not to wait on that, they immediately proceeded to try to alienate from Jesus the supporters who stood in the way of his destruction. And so they sent to Jesus a company of the Pharisees and of the Herodians that they might thus catch him in his talk. (These Herodians had probably come up from Galilee to follow through the hostile purpose they had formed there, as stated in Mark 3: 6.) This new company approaches Jesus with words of hypocritical flattery of his standing as a teacher, his candor, and his courage, and asks him the deadly question, "Is it lawful to give tribute unto Cæsar, or not? Shall we give, or shall we not give?"

Another Question: Tribute

In the first days of Roman domination, the Jerusalem authorities themselves had declared such tribute to be unlawful; and, though they had later accommodated themselves to it, Judas, the Galilean, had made it a battle cry of his revolt, and the Zealots and the Galileans generally were still bitterly opposed to it. But the Pharisees, in keeping with their traditional attitude of political passivity, were largely indifferent to such a matter, provided only that they might enjoy religious liberty. Their program for promoting the coming of the Messianic kingdom and the deliverance of the people did not include political action, or armed revolt, but was based solely upon the most scrupulous observance of the Law as a prerequisite to the divine (apocalyptic) intervention in their behalf. Consequently, if Jesus should now answer their question in the affirmative, he would cease

Its Danger

149

to be, in this grave particular, the popular opponent of the Pharisees and, at the same time, he would inevitably alienate the more militant and "patriotic" element of his supporters. But if he should answer in the negative, he would side with this militant party, and his very popularity would the more expose him to Roman judgment as a dangerous insurrectionist.

The question thus bristled with difficulties; for it really involved a definition of Jesus' Messiahship and mission which it was practically impossible to give to the satisfaction either of his unfriendly questioners or of his enthusiastic but misunderstanding followers. For religiously Jesus was profoundly opposed to the Pharisees; but politically, and, in a measure, apocalyptically, he was at one with them. He agreed with them that deliverance must come from God; but he differed with them profoundly as to the necessary preparation for this deliverance and consequently as to the content of this deliverance when effected. On the other hand, he agreed with the people in the desire for deliverance; but deliverance for him was primarily religious, while for them it was primarily political. His activity for promoting deliverance was in one field; theirs was prone to be in another. He could not worship the devil to attain all the kingdoms of the world; they would scarcely understand such scruples. They could understand an appeal to force; they might accept an apocalyptic promise; but in neither case would they understand or accept the central religious motives and values of Jesus. And the tensity of the situation was such that there was little hope of making these distinctions clear or acceptable to any class of Jesus' followers.

And Difficulty

In his answer, Jesus took the general position of the Pharisees on the issue involved. He would have it understood, at whatever risk, that he was not the **Jesus' Answer** champion of a political program, the fomenter of an armed insurrection. The nature of his Messiahship demanded clarity on that point. And it was a matter of great importance to his followers of later times, as when Mark wrote, as defining the attitude of their Master and themselves to the Roman power. The political inoffensiveness of the Christian movement, its loyal acceptance of the prevailing political order, was demonstrated both for his contemporaries and for later generations by this attitude of Jesus when the question of the tribute was specifically answered by him.

"Why make ye trial of me?" he said to his questioners; "bring me a denarius (shilling), that I may see it." And when it was brought, he called attention to the fact that the coin bore the name and bust of Cæsar. Here then, he intimates, is the Roman money in common circulation among us, and that itself indicates a situation that we cannot deny and need not resist. For this tribute need not be regarded as a sign of ignominious servitude. It may better be regarded as a return to the emperor of that which is his own, and a return in the way of just payment for services rendered in our peace and protec-
Unto Cæsar tion and public order. "Render, therefore, unto Cæsar the things that are Cæsar's." And this was an answer that would block, in this matter, the contemplated charge of sedition, and would satisfy any but the most irreconcilable of Jesus' followers. But it could not satisfy the political agitator or militant Messianist, and it threw the whole burning question of the

coming kingdom of David either into the purely religious or into the purely apocalyptic area, and neither of these aspects was likely long to hold the enthusiasm of the multitude: the religious, because it was too subtle and inward; the apocalyptic, because every day's delay would increase questioning and deepen disappointment. Despite the wisdom and sanity of this part of Jesus' answer, and despite its success in blocking the immediate purpose of his questioners, it is probable that it aroused a feeling of uncertainty, if not of division, among his followers that would tend increasingly to depress the general enthusiasm and to enhance the opposition of the more seriously disappointed among them.

But Jesus did not stop with the question of the tribute to Cæsar. He is not content merely to defend himself from the attack of his enemies; he will turn the situation to their exposure and discomfort. To render to Cæsar the things that are his is only one part, and the lesser part, of the duty of this people, and, in particular, of the duty of his questioners. While they are so concerned about the tribute to Cæsar and are advocates of its payment, they are but little concerned about that higher tribute that they owe to God. They should also "render unto God the things that are God's"; and this his ques-

Unto God

tioners, especially the Pharisees, as the leaders and professedly more religious among them, were not doing, as was amply evidenced by their present treacherous and hypocritical enterprise against himself. And yet this is the ultimate tribute, and its withholding is the ultimate disloyalty. Compared with this, the Cæsar question is transient and insignificant. Render

152

unto Cæsar, indeed, the things that are his; but the more scrupulously render unto God the things that are God's.

After this delegation has withdrawn, a company of the Sadducees approaches Jesus with another sort of question.

Another Question: The Resurrection

They deny the resurrection (which the Pharisees believe in), and they want to know of Jesus whether their view is not sustained both by the Law and by the very necessities of the case. And so they lay before him a hypothetical case, extreme, indeed, but possible. Moses commanded, said they, citing Deuteronomy 25: 5, that if a married man die childless, his brother should marry the widow and raise up seed for the one deceased, so that his name should not perish out of Israel. Here, now, were seven brothers. Under the requirement of this law, each had in turn the one and the same woman as his wife. Finally all the men died, leaving no seed; and last of all the woman also died. In the resurrection, whose wife will this woman be?

This seems to have been one of the stock arguments of the Sadducees in their debate against the Pharisees on the question of the resurrection. Its point is twofold. In regard to the Law, if Moses had believed in a resurrection would he have made such arrangements for the perpetuation of the seed and name of a man in Israel? Would he not have understood that death is but a transient thing, and that the man himself would resume his place in the community in the resurrection? No one would make such provision for an absentee, whose return is really expected. And in regard to its necessary consequences, such a provision, if there were a resurrection, would introduce the utmost confusion in the resur-

Its Point

153

rection state. Was Moses such a man as either to over-
look this fact or deliberately to provide for such confusion?
"The only solution for this difficulty," said they, "consistent with the authority and intelligence of our great
Lawgiver, is that Moses did not believe or teach this doctrine of the resurrection. What, now, is your position in
this matter?"

That this question was intended to embarrass Jesus is
evident; but just how this result was to be accomplished
is not so clear. His questioners certainly ex-
Is Jesus a
Pharisee?   pected him to take the position that there is a
resurrection, and perhaps they thought it
worth while to set up another claim, for themselves and
their adherents, that Jesus' teaching was contrary to
that of Moses. The fact that, in this matter, his position
would be that of the Pharisees would, indeed, give him a
certain standing and protection; but it might also give
occasion for the sneer that this champion of the common
people was himself just a Pharisee, as indicated both here
and in the preceding question concerning the tribute
money.

But this question is not unrelated to the central theme
of this controversy in the temple, the Messiahship of
Jesus and the impending Messianic kingdom. For those
who believed in the resurrection expected the dead to rise
and have their share in that kingdom. Hence Jesus, as
the Messiah, ought to be able to resolve this question of
the Sadducees and tell them how the returned dead, in
the case supposed, would be related to one another without confusion in his kingdom. If he could not do that, how
could he be the Messiah? Indeed, if he could not answer
154

this question, how could he be even as great a Teacher as he was popularly held to be?

Perhaps this last was the main idea in the minds of the Sadducees. They would expose Jesus as an undependable teacher, taking a position that he could not explain or defend in the light of a simple and natural question; and thus they would bring him into disrepute and make a breach between him and his admirers.

But, however they expected to embarrass Jesus, the situation they created was of great significance for the later Church as well as for the contemporaries of Jesus. For it gave him an opportunity both to defend the cardinal Christian doctrine of the resurrection and to interpret it in terms less crass and sensual than those of his questioners, and of the Jewish teaching generally. (Compare Paul's most elaborate interpretation of this doctrine in the fifteenth chapter of First Corinthians.)

In his answer, Jesus tells them that the very form of their question exposes their error and their ignorance,

Jesus' Answer

both of the Scriptures and of the power of God. For the resurrection order is different from the present order. In it there is no marriage, so that questions of marital relations do not arise, and consequently the confusion supposed cannot occur.[2] And the very Scriptures to which the Sadducees refer, if they would look more deeply into them and understand them better, indicate that there is a resurrection.

---

[2]This seems to mean that marriage relations established in this world order become indifferent and are ignored in the order of the resurrection. But it should be remembered that the Sadducean caricature of the resurrection was sensual, not spiritual; so that this teaching does not cover that sweet sympathy and fusion of spirits that characterizes the high and noble marriage. The continuance

For God is a living God, and the God of the living. And so, when we find him describing himself to Moses at the burning bush as "the God of Abraham, and the God of Isaac, and the God of Jacob," we are to understand that these patriarchs, though long dead as men define death, are in fact still living, for "he is not the God of the dead, but of the living."

Jesus makes no specific connection between this proposition and the resurrection from the dead. He simply assures the Sadducees that these patriarchs, as the Scriptures themselves indicate, have not perished. Though they have been so long dead, they are somewhere, somehow, alive to God and recognized by him as his own. But he intends this proposition to be a proof of the resurrection. "As touching the dead, that they are raised," he says. And the inference to be drawn is that, since the patriarchs are alive, their ultimate resurrection is to be expected. They have not lost their share in the promises and hope of Israel. When, therefore, that hope shall be realized in the establishment of the Messianic kingdom, these earliest recipients of the promises, whom God has kept alive against that day, shall return to take their places in it. "These all died in faith, not having received the promises, but having seen them and greeted them from afar, and having confessed that they were strangers and pilgrims on the earth.... And these all, having had witness borne to them through their faith, received not the

Its Implications

of that spiritual relationship in the resurrection state we confidently anticipate. But what Jesus means to teach is that the resurrection does not introduce that high carnival of "pleasures" which the Eastern imagination has so often painted as its chief characteristic and allurement.

156

promise, God having provided some better thing concerning us, that apart from us they should not be made perfect." (Heb. 11: 13, 39, 40.) "But we would not have you ignorant, brethren, concerning them that fall asleep; that ye sorrow not, even as the rest, who have no hope. ... For this we say unto you by the word of the Lord, that we that are alive, that are left unto the coming of the Lord, shall in no wise precede them that are fallen asleep; ... (but) the dead in Christ shall rise first; then we that are alive, that are left, shall together with them be caught up in the clouds, to meet the Lord in the air: and so shall we ever be with the Lord." (1 Thess. 4: 13–17.) These two quotations indicate the line of Jesus' argument.

This argument would naturally meet the approval of the Pharisees, since it defended their own position on the resurrection; but they would scarcely now be disposed to acknowledge anything good in Jesus. But the Pharisees were not all bad, and were not all murderously hostile to Jesus. Some of them were both more liberal in their own views and more generous-minded toward others than the leaders of their party, and to them the teachings of Jesus made strong appeal and for them Jesus had due regard. Their presence, indeed, might afford some ground of hope that the Pharisaic opposition could be withstood or broken. And even though they were not able to change the attitude of their party, or control the issue of events, their presence is worthy of record, especially for its pedagogic and apologetic value as showing that some, at least, of those who were learned in the Law were in sympathy with Jesus. (Compare Joseph of Arimathea, "a councillor of honorable estate" (Mark 15: 43); and, especially, see John 7: 45–52, and 19: 38, 39. See also Acts 5: 33–39.)

One of this group, a scribe, had heard Jesus' answer to the question of the Sadducees and knew that he had answered them well. There was certainly nothing in this answer to account for the hostility of the Pharisees to this Galilean Teacher. Perhaps another question will bring to light the difficulty, or serve for the further vindication of Jesus. And so the scribe asks him, "What (sort of) commandment is the first of all?"

The Scribe's Question

This question calls for a qualitative distinction within the field of the commandments, not necessarily the specification of any particular commandment as first of all; and the sort of distinction he has in mind may be seen in his own contrast between the law of love and the law of sacrifices (Mark 12: 32, 33). But in his answer Jesus both makes the qualitative distinction and specifies the commandments in which that distinction appears. He gives the primacy to the law of love: that is the first commandment of all. This love has two related objects, God and one's neighbor. And for the law of love to God Jesus cites the opening words of the Shema (Deut. 6: 4, 5), "which was recited twice every day by every pious Jew and formed a part of every act of synagogue worship": "Hear, O Israel; The Lord our God, the Lord is one: and thou shalt love the Lord thy God with all thy heart, and with all thy soul, and with all thy mind, and with all thy strength"; while for the law of love for one's neighbor he cites Leviticus 19: 18, "Thou shall love thy neighbor as thyself." "There is none other commandment greater than these."

Jesus' Answer

The scribe again approves the answer of Jesus; and in his comment, consciously or unconsciously, exposes the fundamental difference between Jesus and the leaders of the Pharisees. "Such an attitude of love toward God and one's fellows," says he, "is much more than all whole burnt offerings and sacrifices"; how much more, then, than the lesser elements of the Law or than the traditions of the elders! But the Pharisees were interpreting both God and neighbor in terms of the minutiæ of ritual observance. In such things, for them, the love for God found expression; and those only were their "neighbors" who took the same view and followed the same practices. And this perversion of religious values, with its consequences, underlies the whole controversy between them and Jesus.

But here is one scribe who, in word at least, takes sides with Jesus. "And when Jesus saw that he answered discreetly, he said unto him, Thou art not far from the kingdom of God." What yet separated him from that kingdom we are not told. Perhaps it was that his understanding and his actual attitude did not coincide, so that he would not break with his party, that he knew to be wrong, and become an actual follower of Jesus, whom he knew to be right.

"And no man after that durst ask him any question." Jesus' hostile critics have been put to silence and one of the scribes has even openly expressed his approval. And so the controversy in the temple is brought to a close with his complete and invincible mastery of the situation. His enemies will have to seek some other method of compassing his destruction.

But for a little while Jesus continues his teaching in the

temple. And the first matter that he touches is connected with the burning question of his Messiahship, and may reflect what he knew was still going on in the minds and activities of his enemies, their adverse discussions of the Davidic salutation with which he had been greeted upon his triumphal entry into Jerusalem: "Blessed is the kingdom that cometh, the kingdom of our father David." It may be that they were saying, "This man is not the son of David and therefore cannot be the Messiah"; and this, not necessarily as a matter of genealogy, but because of his appearance, program, and mode of manifestation. "Whether he is David's son by descent or not," say they, "he is certainly not the Son of David who is to be the Messiah, because he fulfills none of the requirements anticipated of such a son. David's Messianic son will be like David, a warrior, a king, a restorer of the kingdom unto Israel; but this man is evidently none of these things."

"Son of David"

And so Jesus raises the question of Messiah's Davidic sonship. "How say the scribes that the Christ is the son of David?" he says, not addressing the question to any particular individual, but reflecting the argument of the scribes against him. And he answers by citing the first verse of the 110th Psalm, which was commonly regarded as Messianic: "The Lord (Jehovah) said unto my Lord (Messiah), Sit thou on my right hand, Till I make thine enemies the footstool of thy feet." "David himself," says Jesus, "here calls the Messiah his Lord: how then can the Messiah be his son?"

The evident purpose of this argument was to discount and correct some element in the scribal interpretation of the Davidic sonship of the Messiah. Jesus might have

160

Not in the
Common
Sense

reminded his hearers that poverty and obscurity were not genealogically inconsistent with such descent, which they would have had to admit in the light of Hillel's undisputed claim to such descent. But even if he had established his genealogical descent from David, which was the accepted belief in the early Church, he would not have met the situation; for not all sons of David could be the Messianic Son, and in the scribal interpretation and the popular expectation Davidic sonship for the Messiah meant Davidic likeness. And it is to that point, therefore, that Jesus' argument is directed. Messiah is not David's son in that sense; for, when David calls him Lord in the Psalm quoted, it is evident from the rest of the quotation that he does not have in mind Messiah's preëminence in the same way and in the same field in which David himself was eminent; but Messiah's recognized preëminence lies in his relation to Jehovah. He is to sit at Jehovah's right hand, while Jehovah reduces his enemies to submission. Any opposition to Jesus, therefore, on the ground that he is not David's Messianic son because he is not like David, is overcome by the fact that David himself recognized this unlikeness. He did not expect Messiah to be like himself, but recognized so deep a difference that he even called Messiah his Lord.

This, then, if we have read the situation aright, is Jesus' answer to an unrecorded criticism of himself. In it we may hear an echo of the whispered insinuations or open debates with which the temple was filled. Though his critics dared no longer come to Jesus openly, they were still busy in their efforts to discredit him and alienate

11   161

his followers. But as yet "the common people (the great multitude) heard him gladly."

And then Jesus proceeds in very caustic and searching words to warn his hearers to be on their guard against these scribes, with their false values, their mean and conceited ambitions, their hypocrisy, and their heartlessness. They are certainly not objects of admiration, imitation, or confidence. They want to be set off, separated, from the common people, measuring their greatness by this separation; and even poor widows who have trusted them and listened to their counsel have found themselves in want, while what should have been their living has been devoted, under the advice of these scribes, to so-called religious uses. But in the coming day these scribes shall be exposed for what they are. Instead of reward from God, they shall receive the greater condemnation—greater than those who do, perhaps, the same things, but do not disguise them under the hypocritical pretenses of religion. These scribes "devour widows' houses" by taking advantage of the widows' desires to be religious, to do something to promote the cause of religion among the people; and the scribes measure the contribution by its mass. It must be a substantial sum to attract their interest and win their approval. Their act is despicable, their standard of values mean and base.

And as Jesus sat opposite the trumpet-shaped receptacles into which the worshipers cast their gifts, he saw men of wealth casting in considerable sums; and in the throng he saw a poor widow with two of the smallest coins in her hand, "two mites," worth about one-fourth of a cent each, and she

Beware of the Scribes

The Widow's Mites

162

cast them both into the nearest receptacle. Perhaps she had been impoverished by the heartless practice of the scribes. Certainly she exhibited the deep devotion of which that practice took advantage. But now she would be of no interest to those who measured gifts by the mass and not by the spirit of them. Her little gift would pass unnoticed or despised. But not so with Jesus. He called his disciples, and told them that the poor widow had cast more than any of the rest into the treasury: "for they all did cast in of their superfluity; but she of her want did cast in all that she had, even all her living." And the gift of all, however small the mass, is more than the gift of part, however great; for God measures the gift not by its size, but by the degree of self-sacrificing devotion that it expresses. His standards are not the world's standards, nor the standards of these "religious" leaders which Jesus would fain correct for his disciples.

163

CHAPTER X

IMPENDING DOOM

MARK 13: 1–37

IF Jesus had any hope that the leaders in Jerusalem would accept him as the Messiah, that hope was dissipated by these controversies in the temple, and those darker forebodings with which he had turned his face toward the city were reawakened and confirmed. He had offered himself to the city; but those who had charge of the religious machinery and policies of the nation would have none of him. On the contrary, his course, especially in the matters of the triumphal entry and the cleansing of the temple, had only intensified their hostility and strengthened their purpose to do away with him. He had, indeed, won popular favor in Jerusalem, as in Galilee; but that made him only the more menacing a figure, at once arousing the envy and increasing the anxiety of the Pharisees and the Sadducees. That favor afforded him a measure of protection from his enemies; but, as he would not turn it to political purposes or a program of violence, it had no further immediate value, and, since its ground was largely defective, it might fail or even be reversed when the hopes on which it was based were disappointed. The appeal to Jerusalem was therefore a failure, and nothing was left for Jesus' vindication but the immediate intervention of God.

Jesus had foreseen this situation, and had already indicated it, chiefly in terms of his own death and resurrec-

164

tion (but see, also, 8: 38–9: 1). Since his ar-
Conse-
quences rival in Jerusalem, he has enlarged these forecasts, in the cursing of the fig tree and the
parable of the wicked husbandmen, to include the divine
judgment and rejection of that system and that leadership which would not receive him, but was determined
to put him to death. Now, at the close of these controversies in the temple, which had not issued in the conviction but had disclosed the final obduracy of the religious leaders, he turns again to the future and contemplates what it has in store both for his enemies and, especially, for his friends.

As Jesus and his disciples went out of the temple at
the close of the day, one of the disciples called his atten-
The Temple tion to the size of the stones and the general
magnificence of the structure. The temple
was, indeed, one of the remarkable buildings of the world,
and its size and splendor made a profound impression
upon all who saw it, much more, then, upon these provincial Galileans. But it was not an alien's wonder
and admiration to which they now gave expression.
For they were Jews, and the temple had long been the
center and symbol of Jewish religious life and loyalty.
It was not merely an impressive building: to the Jew it
was a sacred building whose splendor served only fitly to
express its sacredness. And so the disciples' wonder had
in it a certain pride of nationalism and an element of religious sentiment and reverence.

Jesus, too, saw the beauty of the structure; but to him
it was a hollow sham, a tragic delusion. It was not the
To Jesus dwelling place of the Most High. It was not
the source of instruction in the knowledge of

165

God for the Chosen People, not to mention the Gentiles.
On the contrary, it had become the stronghold of Sad-
duceeism and Pharisaism, the center of a heartless and
worldly priestcraft and an equally heartless and pompous
hypocrisy; and so it represented an interpretation of God
and religion utterly repugnant to all that Jesus was and
stood for. And in proportion as it held the loyalty of the
people, it not only gave them perverse instruction, but
it stood in the way of anything better.

Such a system must be reformed or destroyed; and if
the temple was its bulwark, it too must be destroyed.
For his own name's sake, and for his people's
Its Destruction sake, God would change this situation. And
since change by reform was now evidently impossible,
God would soon bare his arm for judgment and destruction. Such was Jesus' insight and indomitable faith.
And so when the disciples invited him to join in their
admiration of the temple, he told them, surely with
a touch of sadness in his indignation, that this temple
should be utterly destroyed: "There shall not be left
here one stone upon another, which shall not be thrown
down."

Such a prediction of the destruction of the temple was
not without precedents in the prophetic history of Israel.[1]
It has, indeed, been called one of "the axioms
Axioms of Prophecy of prophecy" that whatever stood in the way
of the realization of the divine purpose for
the establishment of righteousness should be destroyed,
and righteousness was interpreted by the prophets not
in terms of cult and its ritual, but in terms of character and social contacts. To the devotee of the cult,

---

[1]See Amos, chapters 5 and 6; Isaiah 6: 11ff.; Jeremiah 24.

of course, especially to those who lived by it, the cult
seemed supreme and its preservation essential to the
integrity of religion and the honor of God; and any criticism of the cult, much more the prophecy of its destruction, seemed the height of blasphemous disloyalty. But
to the prophet character was supreme, and the worth of
the cult lay in its fitness truly to represent the character
of Jehovah and to foster a like character in his worshipers;
and whenever the cult failed at this crucial point, it and
its instruments must be, and would be, destroyed for the
honor of God and the promotion of his righteousness.
Not only the temple, but the sacred city of Jerusalem
would be destroyed, the Holy Land laid waste, and the
Chosen People decimated and disciplined by captivity
and exile that the character of Jehovah might be vindicated and his righteousness established among men.

This deep and ancient controversy between the prophet
and the cult came to a head again in the days of Jesus,
and reached its climax with his ministry in Jerusalem.
The leaders of the cult took their traditional attitude
toward him, and he responded with pronouncements of
judgment similar to those of the ancient prophets. (Compare Mark 14: 57, 58; Acts 6: 14, and 21: 28.)

After his declaration that the temple, despite its magnificence, should be destroyed, because it did not promote,
but hindered, the righteous purpose of God,
When? Jesus and the disciples went on their way to
the Mount of Olives, where, probably, they would spend
the night. And as he sat in the dusk on the hillside, looking sadly across toward that splendid building whose ruin
he had foretold, the four of his disciples who were his most
intimate friends, Peter and James and John and Andrew,

167

asked him privately: "Tell us, when shall these things be? and what shall be the sign when these things are all about to be accomplished?"

This question seems to indicate ("these things . . . all these things") that Jesus had told the disciples more of the future than the single fact of the coming destruction of the temple; but they still want more specific information as to the time of the coming events, and so they ask him when the events foretold are going to take place, and what is to be the sign by whose appearance they may know that the time is at hand. And it is this request for "the sign" that dominates the answer of Jesus.

The Sign

His answer falls into the usual threefold form of contemporary Jewish apocalypses—The Travail; The Tribulation; The Appearance—each division marking a stage in the expected deliverance of the Chosen People. (Compare Hosea 13: 13; Isaiah 66: 7–9; Micah 4: 9, 10.) Here the "Chosen People" are the followers of Jesus; and the main concern of his discourse is their guidance and protection through the troubled times that are just before them. They must know how to read "the signs" aright, lest they be deceived; what to expect for themselves, lest they be discouraged; and what to do that they may be saved from the general destruction.

1. "The beginning of travail" will be the appearance of false Christs, leading many astray, wars and rumors of wars, and famines and pestilences. But the disciples are not to be deceived by these things, for they are only the beginnings, "but the end is not yet." And the foreknowledge of these things and of their place in the unfolding future will promote sobriety

Travail

168

and self-control on the part of the disciples and protect them against excessive and misplaced Messianic and eschatological enthusiasms. It is a counsel of calmness.

But for themselves, even in this period of beginnings, believers are to expect persecutions of all sorts, public and private; but the Holy Spirit will help them to make defense when they are brought to trial. They will be hated by all men as the followers of Jesus; but he that endureth to the end—the consummation, the Parousia (as indicated above)—shall be saved, shall have his part in that glorious event. But the end will not come until the gospel has first been preached to all the nations.

The spread of the gospel among the Gentiles will thus be another sign of the times. They need not all accept it, but they must all have the chance, before the present world era is brought to an end. (Compare Romans 11: 25, 26.) Until that preliminary condition has been fulfilled the end is not to be expected. That the end will follow quickly the fulfillment of the condition may be inferred, but is not stated. And, in any case, believers must not be deceived or carried away with excessive apocalyptic enthusiasm before that condition has been fulfilled. This, too, is a counsel of calmness.

2. But the days of tribulation will soon follow, and they will be introduced by the appearance of "the abomination of desolation" standing where he **Tribulation** ought not. This Danielic phrase (Daniel 12: 11) is the key to the sign that is now given; and so Mark introduces a word of warning of the importance of its proper understanding, "Let him that readeth understand." In Daniel, the phrase describes the altar of Zeus Ouranios which Antiochus Epiphanes erected in

169

the temple in 167 B.C., the Zeus Ouranios, "Lord of Heaven," being contemptuously translated "Abomination of Desolation." And so some interpreters think, especially since Mark describes the Abomination as "he," that the present reference is to the threatened setting up of the statue of the Roman emperor in the temple for the worship of the Jews, emperor worship being the Roman state religion and participation in it an evidence of loyalty to the Roman authority. This certainly was apt to happen in any revolt of the Jews that centered in the national religion and the exclusive worship of Jehovah.

But other interpreters see in "the abomination that makes desolate" the army of the Romans, who, as Tacitus says, "make a desert, and call it peace"; and in "standing where he ought not" they see the presence of that army on the sacred soil of the Holy Land, where a Gentile army should not be. And so Luke says, "But when ye see Jerusalem compassed with armies, then know that her desolation is at hand" (Luke 21: 20), retaining and making specific the word "desolation," but omitting the "abomination" of the Danielic phrase. So he obeyed the Marcan injunction, "Let him that readeth understand"; and many, perhaps most, interpreters have followed him. In this view the reference is to the revolt of the Jews in 66 A.D. that culminated in the destruction of Jerusalem and the temple in 70 A.D. and was attended with indescribable horrors both within the city and outside in Judæa. "Then shall be the tribulation," and tribulation without parallel. And that shall be the sign for instant action on the part of believers—not, indeed, to resist the desolating abomination and to join in the futile effort to save Judæa and Jerusalem from the merited doom that overshadows them, but to save themselves by hurried flight. "Let him that is on the housetop not go down, nor enter in, to take anything out of his house; and let him that is in the field not return back to take his cloak." (Mark 13: 15, 16.)

So swift and terrible will this judgment be that it will threaten the destruction of the whole population of Judæa, believer and unbeliever alike. But the believer will have two advantages: he is forewarned of the issue, and so will not be involved in the fatal delusion of resistance; and for his sake God himself will shorten the days of the tribulation, reduce their number, so that all may not be indiscriminately destroyed.

But not even then are they to expect the second coming of Christ. In the distress and confusion of the times pretenders, indeed, will appear in response to troubled expectations and delusive hopes of deliverance. There will be false prophets and false Christs, doing signs and wonders, and deceiving many; and many will say, "Lo, here is the Christ; or, Lo, there"; but whether these be Jews who, having denied the Christhood of Jesus, see in someone else their Messianic deliverer, or whether they be believers carried away by excess of enthusiasm for his own second coming, the understanding believer, forewarned, will not be deceived by them. His own second coming is not of this sort; and it will be preceded by signs of a different order, which cannot be mistaken. Them they are to await with patient watchfulness and readiness.

Up to this point Jesus' discourse has dealt with the earthly and human events that culminated with the destruction of Jerusalem and the temple in 70 A.D., and the tendency of the discourse has been to restrain the apocalyptic enthusiasm of his followers and to warn them against the Messianic delusions that lay so close at hand in the tragic course of imminent events. He has not yet answered the disciples' question, "When shall these things be?" but he has given them a series of "signs" that should precede his prophecy of the destruction of the temple, along with warnings and instructions for their guidance as these signs appeared.

3. But now he takes up the question of the time, and passes from the destruction of Jerusalem to his own second coming, the Parousia. It, too, should be preceded by signs, but signs of a different order from those already enumerated. "But in those days, after that tribulation, there shall be dreadful disturbances in the heavens: the sun and the moon shall not give their light, the stars shall fall, and the powers that are in the heavens (whether the constellations themselves, or the spiritual beings that dwell in the heavens[2]) shall be shaken." "And then shall they see the Son of man coming in clouds with power and great glory," and the elect from all the earth shall be separated and gathered together unto him.

The Coming

Like the fig tree forecasts the coming of summer, so shall these signs forecast the coming of the Son of man; and as you know from the budding of the fig tree that the summer is not far away, so shall you know from these signs that the coming of the Son of man is near. But the

---

[2]"The spiritual hosts of wickedness in the heavenly places," says Paul (Eph. 6: 12). In this sense, the allusion would be to Jesus' controversy and final victory over these hosts of evil.

exact day and hour is not known even to the Son of man himself. Only the Father knows that.

And if the Son does not know it, neither can his followers. But the Son's departure may be likened to the **Watch** case of a householder going to sojourn in another country. As he turns over his affairs to his servants and bids the porter be on the watch for his return, so now the Son, about to go away, bids his servants be on the watch, "lest coming suddenly he find you sleeping." And this injunction is not limited to the apostles only; it applies to all believers. They are all to be on the watch against that day.

And so Jesus answers the double question of the four disciples: "When shall these things be?" and "What **Wait** shall be the sign?" The question, as we have seen, originated in the prediction of the destruction of the temple; but the answer passes beyond that to the consummation of the age and the coming of the Son of man. As to the time, it is not immediate,[3] and its exact day and hour cannot be known. In the interval, the disciples are not to be deceived by pretenders or by their own misreading of the "signs"; they are not to lose their confidence in the events by reason of the delay; but they are to be both patient and watchful, for the events will certainly take place. And as to the signs, they, when they appear, will be unmistakable. No merely human disturbances will immediately precede and herald that last great day of the coming of the Son of man. It shall be preceded and ushered in by cosmic disorders which only the hand of God can produce. Until

[3]Compare, "They supposed that the kingdom of God was immediately to appear" (Luke 19: 11).

these appear, the disciples must be patient, steadfast in their faith; watching for their appearance, indeed, but neither doubtful nor disturbed. And when such signs do appear, they may know that their patient watchfulness is to be rewarded, for their "redemption draweth nigh" (see Luke 21: 28).

174

CHAPTER XI

THE SHADOW OF DEATH

MARK 14: 1–42

THE discourse on the course of history up to Jesus' second coming in triumph has carried us far ahead of the narrative of the Master's earthly life. It recognizes the finality of the temple scenes in Jesus' appeal to the nation, and it assumes his death as a consequence of the failure of that appeal. He will have, indeed, a vindication in his resurrection, in the judgment that is soon to come upon the nation that rejected him, and in his second coming with power and great glory; but that vindication will not hinder—indeed, it will be won by—his death at the hands of his enemies. Such is his Father's program, both for himself and for the redemption of the people through him.

Connection

It remains, therefore, to relate the closing scenes of his earthly life, and the first stage of his vindication in his resurrection. And so the narrative now returns to the temple scenes, and resumes the thread of the story with their consequences. And these consequences are to be attached not primarily to the several controversies recorded, but rather to the initial scene of the temple cleansing. For that was Jesus' only overt act against established authority, and it consolidated against him the hostility of the Sadducean priestly hierocracy, whose control it challenged and set at naught, and was thus the immediate cause of his execution. For this group now took over the leadership of the opposition which, in Galilee, had found its chief representatives among the local Pharisees.

It was, therefore, the chief priests, Sadducean leaders, and the scribes of the Pharisees who now "sought how they might take him with subtlety, and kill him." "With subtlety," since it was pass-over time, and the city was crowded, and they feared a tumult of the people because of the popularity of Jesus; and a tumult, if it did not directly dislodge them, would certainly invite the intervention of the Roman authority, with consequences that, whether from patriotic or from selfish motives (since they held office by Roman favor), they might well desire to avoid.

Plot of the
Leaders

This proposal of violence is not new. It has underlain all the preceding narrative from the emergence of Jesus as a public and popular figure. But now it has a new, more powerful, and more deadly leadership, and more plausible material on which to operate. For Jesus has now openly assumed a Messianic rôle, and, as the Messiah, has said and done things that may easily, with a little ingenuity, be turned to his destruction. But still, as hitherto, his popularity as the leader and champion of the people must be reckoned with and countered; and that consideration probably determined his enemies' course. Assassination, tried more than once in the case of Paul, or mob murder, tried in Paul's case, and successful in the case of Stephen, was evidently here unwise, and, to an extent, impracticable because of the caution of Jesus. His death would have to be compassed with some degree of regularity and behind some protective cover; and that pointed directly to the Roman court, which alone had the authority to execute a capital sentence and the power to do it safely.

Jesus is not ignorant of his danger, nor indifferent to it. He has foreseen his death as a part of his Father's plan for the bringing in of the kingdom, and has **Jesus' Situation** come up to Jerusalem in loyal self-dedication to his Father's will. And now the certainty and imminence of death occupy his mind and color all the last hours of his intercourse with his friends. For all that remains to him is to prepare himself and them for the coming end.

That even he needed such final preparation is indicated by Gethsemane. The disciples' need is written all over the record. They have not yet accepted the idea of his death, much less entered into his understanding of it. They are already under strain, how shall they face the impending crisis? What more can he do to prepare them for it, to show them its place and meaning in the providence of God, so that something, at least, of their faith and hope may survive the shock, and they may not be overwhelmed by it as by final and irretrievable disaster?

These are the questions that underlie Jesus' last hours with his disciples. There is now an especial emphasis upon his foreknowledge of the coming events, designed both to exhibit his supernatural character and particularly to show that these events did not take him by surprise and so make of his death an unexpected and an unwilling tragedy. Based upon this certainty of death, we have, therefore, (1) its effect upon the disciples, **The Problem** and (2) Jesus' final efforts to make them understand it as he does and to encourage

12   177

them with his own assurance that it is not the end but rather the beginning of the kingdom of God.

Jesus is, indeed, for the moment safe in Bethany, where apparently he spent Wednesday in retirement with his friends. Here, in the house of an otherwise unknown Simon, the leper, whom Jesus at an earlier time may have restored to health and home, a certain woman of substance, perhaps a daughter of the house, anoints his head, as he reclined at table, with very pure and very precious ointment. In this gracious act this woman expresses her devotion to Jesus, perhaps her estimate of him as the Messiah ("The Anointed"), and the scene might be recorded simply "for a memorial of her." But its place in the narrative and Jesus' treatment of it suggest a deeper connection with the course of events.

Jesus in Bethany

There were some in the company who took the woman sharply to task for what they called her unjustifiable extravagance. For the value of the ointment was considerable, and, to their mind, it might better have been sold and the proceeds have been given to the poor. But Jesus came to the woman's defense on the ground that the peculiar circumstances justified the seeming waste. For he was about to die, and this anointing was really in anticipation of his burial; and certainly the treatment of dying loved ones is exempt from cold and calculating criticism. It has its own standards, set up by love, that a like love will recognize and respect, as will be shown by the lasting memory of this incident.

Some Offended

"And Judas, he that was one of the twelve, went away unto the chief priests, that he might deliver him unto

178

Judas Iscariot them. And they, when they heard it, were glad, and promised to give him money."

As we have seen, there had been something of difference, a potential breaking point, between Jesus and the twelve from the time he began to tell them of his rejection and death. The events of the last few days had not relieved this difficulty. But it took his actual arrest to break down the loyalty of the eleven Galileans among the twelve. Then, but only then, "they all left him, and fled." But even so they had loved him too much either to betray him or to forget him.

Peter's denial is a vivid illustration of the strain of these last days. But Judas, the Judean, broke first and most tragically under this strain, perhaps because of his Judean affiliations; and this scene in Bethany was the last straw, the immediate cause of his defection. He could no longer adhere to a leader who justified waste on the ground of his imminent death. If fear broke down Peter twenty-four hours later, if personal ambition had marred the attitude of James and John, as they drew near to Jerusalem, and these three Jesus' most intimate friends, less wonder that disappointment and disgust broke down Judas first of all. The group broke first at its weakest and remotest point, broke there because of "the offense of the cross," and broke there beyond repair. And Judas "sought how he might conveniently deliver him unto them." Henceforth Jesus has to face not only his open enemies but a determined traitor in his own circle, who has established connection with these open enemies and only waits his opportunity to use his special knowledge of Jesus' movements to deliver him into their hands.

As a consequence, the caution which had led Jesus to

179

withdraw from Jerusalem each night was now redoubled.

Redoubled
CautionFor the impending events were not only a crisis for the disciples, they were a crisis, *the* crisis, for Jesus himself; and as he would not evade the Father's will concerning him, neither would he forestall that will by any act of carelessness or bravado of his own.

And so, when the time came for the eating of the passover, as that must be eaten in Jerusalem and the interests of the rite would largely occupy the minds of the friendly crowds, Jesus took particular precautions to conceal the place in the city where he proposed to eat the meal with his disciples. When they wanted to know where they should make the necessary preparations, Jesus gave them directions that were unintelligible even to the twelve. For he told two of them to go into the city and follow a man who would meet them bearing a pitcher of water. To the master of the house he entered they should say, "The Teacher saith, Where is my guest chamber, where I shall eat the passover with my disciples?" And in the upper room that he would point out the two disciples should make ready for their company.

When evening came—probably after six o'clock on Thursday, as we should say, which would be the beginning of Friday, as they counted the days from Betrayal
Revealedsunset to sunset—Jesus and "the Twelve" (probably used as a general designation, and meaning the ten who had remained with him) came to the place which the two had thus prepared for them. As they ate, Jesus gave them a word of warning and appeal when he revealed the fact that his death would be brought about through the treachery of one of their own number,

180

a treachery the blacker because even at this moment of its plotting the traitor was keeping his place and sharing in their common and sacred meal. In the light of this distressing revelation, perhaps because each one felt that, in some degree, he had not been fully loyal to his Master, they began to ask him, each for himself, "Is it I?" But Jesus gives them no specific information; for "he that dippeth with me in the dish" was not enough to identify Judas, as they all dipped in the common dish as they ate together. He does, however, add a word of solemn judgment. His death was a part of the Father's plan, "even as it is written of him," but that will not absolve the traitor from his personal responsibility and guilt. Rather, Woe unto him: good were it for him if he had not been born!

This stress upon the blackness of the treachery of a friend is not merely an exhibition of Jesus' foreknowledge, not merely a preparation of the rest for that which was to come. It is an appeal to the better nature of them all, lest they should fall into that guilt that they instinctively reprehended, and become the objects of that condemnation that they instinctively approved. It is an appeal for friendship by way of a near and gross example of its abuse, and with the eleven it was not without response or without meaning for the future.

This searching and softening of hearts is good preparation for the supreme lesson that Jesus now endeavors to teach the disciples: the lesson of the meaning and worth of his death as a part of the redemptive plan of God, taught through vivid and appropriate symbol. Taking a loaf of the bread from the table, he broke it, with the customary thanksgiving, and gave the pieces to the disciples with the words, "Take

The Last
Supper

181

ye: this is my body." And then, in the same fashion, he took a cup of the wine and gave it to them to drink, with the fuller words, "This is my blood of the covenant, which is poured out for many."

His disciples are to see in this symbolic act that Jesus' death is a free gift, a deliberate dedication of himself to death for the sake of his people. He lays down his life of himself; no man takes it from him either by surprise or by superior power. His body and blood, his life, are given as the supreme expression of loyalty to God and love for his own. And he has chosen this path because he has seen it as his Father's will, the only way by which his mission may be accomplished, his message vindicated. He is to do by his death what he has not done by his life, so that his death is not the defeat, but the means of the achievement, of his, which is his Father's, purpose. By it he will make atonement for the sins of the people, and thus inaugurate and seal the covenant of a new deliverance for a new and better Israel.

Jesus' death is thus integrally related to his message of the coming kingdom. It is at once the seal of that message and the condition and means of the kingdom's coming. As his whole attitude has been not to be ministered unto, but to minister, so now the giving of his life a ransom for many is the last supreme act of his redemptive ministration. By his death, at last, the kingdom of God will be introduced; and Jesus, who is now at his last supper with this little group of initial members of that kingdom, sees beyond impending separation the coming day when he shall again "drink of the fruit of the vine new in the kingdom of God." And in this confidence he faces death, not as defeat, but as the means of victory.

182

And he would fain have the disciples see the issue as he sees it, so that they may meet it with a like faith and hope.

When the little company left the upper room for their customary resort upon the Mount of Olives, Judas, know-

Judas Goes to the Chief Priests

ing that now the convenient time had come, went to the chief priests and the scribes with information of Jesus' whereabouts and a proposal to guide an arresting party to seize him. (Perhaps a son of the house saw him go, and, suspecting, followed him.)

Jesus and the rest went on their way to the Mount of Olives, and as they went Jesus gave them a final word of warning and of encouragement. He knew

Jesus Goes to the Mount of Olives

that they were not yet ready for the issue they were going to meet, and therefore, when the issue came, they might, they would, abandon him and lose the faith and hope that centered in him. They needed still to be warned against their own, to them unexpected, collapse; and to be assured that it, too, had been foreseen and that, despite its depressing effect, they had not believed and hoped in vain. For he who told them that the collapse would come, contrary to all their expectations, told them also of a restoration and a reunion; so that the coming collapse, confirming Jesus' word, might even serve as a ground of confidence in the realization of his promise.

And so Jesus now tells them that they will all be caused to stumble at the smiting that awaits him;

The Sheep Shall Be Scattered

for is it not written, "I will smite the shepherd, and the sheep shall be scattered"? "Howbeit," he adds for their encouragement, despite the smiting

183

of the shepherd and the scattering of the sheep, "after I am raised up, I will go before you into Galilee." The scattered sheep shall soon be gathered again under their once smitten, but now risen, Shepherd. In their native Galilee, whither he will have preceded them, their broken company shall be reunited. As in the upper room the kingdom is shown beyond the shadow of death, so here reunion is shown beyond impending separation; and in both cases the purpose is the same, to show the disciples that dawn lies beyond the gathering dark.

But They Shall Be Gathered Again

But the disciples do not like, or accept, the forecast of their scattering. And Peter, who naturally and characteristically leads their protest, assures Jesus that, even though alone, he at least will stand with him even unto death. In this assurance he places himself along with James and John, who not long before had assured Jesus that they could drink of his cup and be baptized with his baptism; but neither he nor they were prepared to make their boasting good. "Three times," says Jesus to his protestations — as completely and as emphatically as possible — "thou shalt deny me; and that, too, on this very night on which we have already entered." And thus he repeats and emphasizes, "I will smite the shepherd, and the flock shall be scattered." Peter's defection is representative of this scattering of the flock and emphasizes it. In a wider sense his defection is a part of the complete isolation of Jesus and of the complete "stumbling of Israel" in him. It emphasizes both his utter loneliness and the singularity of his position in regard to the redemptive work that is to

Peter's Denial Foretold

184

be accomplished by his death. And this thought runs over into the next tragic paragraph.

They are now come "unto a place which was named Gethsemane," a small inclosed olive grove somewhere on the western side of the Mount of Olives,

The Mount of Olives a common place of seclusion for Jesus and the disciples, so that Judas, too, would know where to look for him. And here is the first dreadful scene in the smiting of the Shepherd, which

The Shepherd Shall Be Smitten is also the last in Jesus' preparation for his fate.

As they enter the garden, Jesus says to eight of the disciples, "Sit ye here, while I pray." The three intimate and too-boastful ones, Peter and James and John, who alone had been permitted to see the Transfiguration at the beginning of the gospel of his suffering, he takes with him farther into the garden that they may now see something of the meaning and depth of that suffering and may help somewhat by their presence and sympathy in the bearing of it.

It has already been said that Jesus himself needed some final preparation for his death. This is the scene of that preparation, and he is its lonely and central

The Agony in Gethsemane figure. But the chosen three needed their lesson, a lesson of weakness and of the need of watchfulness and prayer; and this is their lesson. And the agony and supreme self-dedication of Jesus, their lesson material, are thrown into higher light by their own behavior, as that too shows their own need of learning. The Transfiguration had been a lesson in the glory of the Lord; Gethsemane is a lesson in that suffering through which he entered into his glory.

185

As Jesus and the three draw away from the others, Jesus "began to be greatly amazed and sore troubled," and said to them: "My soul is exceeding sorrowful even unto death: abide ye here, and watch." In the depth of his sudden and appalling distress he wanted the sympathetic companionship of his friends.

We do not know through what agonies of soul Jesus may already have passed in earlier crises of his life, as in the Temptation, or in the heroic determination to come up to Jerusalem. But we know that he was wont to pray, especially in connection with such crises, and that those prayers were for guidance and help that he might fully know and fully do his Father's will. Here and there in his life, indeed, we catch glimpses of inner pain, of disappointment and distress, and these are intimations of a wider and deeper area than appears upon the surface. But in Gethsemane —not in Gethsemane alone, but in Gethsemane most of all until we come to his cry upon the cross— "though he was a Son, yet learned he obedience by the things which he suffered" (Heb. 5: 8), "becoming obedient even unto death, yea, the death of the cross" (Phil. 2: 8). For his distress had as its immediate impulse the vision of imminent death. He had foreseen it; had, indeed, come to meet it; but now that it is upon him it seems very terrible. He had spoken of the cup that he must drink, but now that it was at his lips he prayed, as perhaps he had prayed before, that it might be removed from him.

We may not eliminate the pain of physical death as an element in our Lord's perplexity and distress, for he was no Stoic, no abnormal seeker for spectacular martyrdom.

186

But certainly that was not the only or the major element; for there was yet opportunity for escape, if to save his life was to be his supreme consideration. That *was a* consideration; and as such it offered its challenge to the supreme consideration, which was to finish his work in accordance with his Father's will.

But not *that* he must die, but *why*, was the major element in his agony. In that lay its supreme temptation. It challenged his willingness to conform to the Father's will because of the mystery of that will—an aspect of the universal mystery of godliness and pain. The kingdom must come; to that he was wholly dedicated. But could it not come in some other way than by his death? Might not the Father, to whom all things were possible, use even yet some other means? Why should this be the only way? But if there were some other way, then his death was not his vindication but his abandonment. "My God, my God, why hast thou forsaken me?" has its anticipations in this agony. And what Jesus sought was the assurance that this was the only way by which the Father's will might be done and his kingdom be ushered in.

And so he prayed three times, "Abba, Father"—the cry of a Son, perplexed, but still a Son—"all things are possible unto thee" (even the bringing in of the kingdom without my death); therefore, "remove this cup from me" (since, in thy power, some other means may serve); "howbeit" (despite the mystery and the pain), "not what I will" (in weakness, perplexity, and distress), "but what thou wilt" (for in thy will is a Father's love and goodness, directing every expression of a Father's power). So did faith rise to its loftiest heights and filial consecration find its sublimest expression. If triumph in earlier tempta-

187

tions was meaningful and glorious, what shall we say of this? That, losing his life, he found it; and, being made perfect through sufferings, "became unto all them that obey him the author of eternal salvation" (Heb. 5: 9).

But the three disciples whose solemn privilege it was to share this scene with their Master, who might, in sympathy at least, have kept him company and shared somewhat his sufferings, had soon fallen asleep, "for their eyes were very heavy." When Jesus turned back to them, after his first petition, seeking that human touch for whose sustaining he had taken them with him, and found them already asleep, he rebuked them, addressing himself particularly to that spirit of vain self-confidence that characterized them all, but had found most recent expression in Peter's protests of undying loyalty, "Simon, sleepest thou? couldest thou not watch one hour?" And then he added an exhortation that throws light upon the situation for himself as well as for them: "Watch ye and pray, that ye enter not into temptation: the spirit indeed is willing, but the flesh is weak." He himself felt this, but he was meeting and overcoming temptation, as was his wont, with watchfulness and prayer. They have a too easy confidence in the flesh, too little realization of the power of temptation, and consequently too little sense of their need of preparation to meet it and of the means by which alone it could be met. Their sleeping lost them largely the lesson of their Master's example, but his words indicated the lesson they needed to learn—the lesson that, so far as they were concerned, was the purpose of their presence upon the scene.

The Sleeping Three

Their Lesson

When he comes to the disciples the third time, and finds them again asleep, Jesus has won his victory, and apparently gives over the fruitless effort for their further instruction. "Apparently": for his words, "Sleep on now, and take your rest," may be read as a profoundly reproachful question, "Do ye sleep on then and take your rest?" (R. V., margin).

Jesus, Victorious, Goes to Meet Judas

In any case, the tragic scene is over. The arresting party, guided by Judas, comes into view. And with the words, "It is enough. . . . Arise, let us be going," Jesus with the three returns to the other disciples to meet the traitor and the band he led.

189

CHAPTER XII

THE SMITING OF THE SHEPHERD

MARK 14: 43–16: 8

WHEN Judas informed the chief priests that the convenient time had now come, he was provided with a band of servants, armed with swords and clubs, for the arrest of Jesus. As Jesus would need identification, being unknown by face to this band of servants, Judas told them that he would identify him for them by giving him the customary salutation of a disciple. With these crude but sufficient preparations he led them to Gethsemane, and there he found Jesus with the other disciples near the entrance of the garden where, as we have seen, they had gathered to meet the arresting party. Judas approached Jesus, as he had so often done before, with the salutation of a disciple to his master. "Rabbi," he said, and took Jesus' hand and kissed it. Whereupon "they laid hands on him, and took him."

Arrest of Jesus

Opposition was evidently expected. But, for Jesus himself, it took only the form of a protest against the manner of his seizure. His career had been public, that of a teacher in the temple. If he had done anything worthy of arrest, why had he not been arrested then and there by the temple police? Why should he now be seized like a robber in the nighttime? But let the Scriptures be fulfilled.

This was not, however, the temper of the crowd. Blows were struck on both sides, and "a certain one of them [of the friends of Jesus] that stood by drew his

190

Resistance sword, and smote the servant of the high priest, and struck off his ear." And this led to a general assault upon the disciples, not to arrest, but to scatter them and prevent the rescue of Jesus; "and they all left him, and fled." But one of Jesus' friends was loath to leave him, a certain young man, not of the Twelve, who had joined the party with only his shawl-like outer garment thrown over his naked body. He had probably come hastily from the home in which the last supper was eaten—perhaps he was John Mark himself—to warn Jesus of his danger, and he lingered with him after the rest had fled. Him the arresting party now sought to seize; but when they laid hold of his garment he left it in their hands and ran away naked. And so Jesus was left quite alone in the hands of his enemies. And, except for Peter and his denial, which only emphasizes the scattering of the sheep and the isolation of the shepherd, the disciples are mentioned no more in this Gospel.[1]

Jesus is immediately led away to the house of the high priest, and arraigned before a special meeting of the San-

Jesus Before the San-hedrin hedrin, hastily assembled there to carry through their purpose of putting him to death. The high priest was the president of this body, whose members were both Pharisees and Sadducees. Both groups, as we have seen, were hostile to Jesus, the one for religious, the other for political reasons; and so now Jesus does not really face a trial, but rather "a hasty concourse (of his avowed enemies) to carry out, with such legal forms as the occasion admits of, *a political murder*" (Menzies). And since the power of life and

---

[1] This, of course, ignores the later supplement, 16: 9-20.

death was with the Roman governor, what the Sanhedrin must have was some plausible case to present to him to induce him to order the execution of Jesus. And that could be found only by showing the political aspects of his activities.

But as a Jewish court they must condemn the prisoner under Jewish law, and then persuade the governor to carry out their sentence by the presentation of the case in its Roman aspects. If the two could be combined, it would be, for them, an ideal combination; because it would at once assure the death of Jesus and exhibit their loyalty to the Roman authorities and their pious zeal to their own people. And Jesus' Messianic claims and behavior opened the door for just this combination.

Under the Jewish law a conviction for blasphemy was ideal for their purpose. Its penalty was death, and it would rally against the condemned the piety
The Charge of
Blasphemy of all the devout. And a charge of blasphemy against Jesus had long been in the air. It had been the first criticism leveled against him by the scribes at the beginning of his ministry (Mark 2: 1–12), and his subsequent course had given it support. And undoubtedly many of the Pharisees and their followers already regarded him as a blasphemer.

But now it seemed impossible to secure adequate testimony against him. With the scrupulosity as to method that frequently characterizes bad men seeking an evil end, and, more frequently and more creditably, men of defective insight who really think the evil end they seek is good, the Sanhedrin sought the concurring testimony of the two witnesses required by the law to prove the charges against Jesus. But, though there were many to testify,

192

the testimony was inconclusive because no two witnesses
were found to agree.

Presently, however, there appeared a plausible charge
that seemed to be sustained: Jesus, it was alleged, had
spoken against the temple. "We heard him say," said
the witnesses, "I will destroy this temple that is made with
hands, and in three days I will build another made without hands."

How dangerous was this charge may be seen from the
later experience of Stephen, against whom the witnesses
testified, "This man ceaseth not to speak
words against this holy place, and the law:
for we have heard him say, that this Jesus of
Nazareth shall destroy this place, and shall change the
customs which Moses delivered unto us" (Acts 6: 13, 14);
and from the case of Paul, who also was charged with
"teaching all men everywhere against the people, and
the law, and this place" (Acts 21: 28; 25: 8). For, since
the temple was the center both of the formal and traditional religious life of the people (though it had largely
been superseded by the synagogue in the simpler religious
life) and of all the national independence and authority
that had been left to the Jewish state, a threat of its destruction was not only an indication of religious radicalism
that could speak lightly of God's house, the place where
his honor dwelt, but was also an intimation of impending
revolution, social and political as well as religious, not,
indeed, against Roman supremacy, but within the order-
ing and control of the Jewish nation itself. It might,
therefore, involve both blasphemy and treason.

Laid against Jesus, the charge was the more serious
because it had a certain support in fact. Worldly wisdom

*Against the
Temple*

13   193

Its Support would perhaps impose a discreet silence upon the Sadducees in regard to his cleansing of the temple; but his preaching of the kingdom had implied some sort of revolution, his whole attitude toward mere institutional and traditional religion had been offensive and revolutionary, and he had begun his apocalyptic discourse (Mark 13) with a specific prophecy of the destruction of the temple. The witnesses had not, indeed, heard that discourse; but they may very well, in the light of what has just been said, have heard something of similar import. But whatever they had heard, whether misunderstood or willfully perverted, their testimony failed here also because of its inconsistency. "Their witness did not agree together."

To all these accusations Jesus made no defense, to the surprise and embarrassment of the court. The charges, indeed, were misrepresentations, willful or **The Silence of Jesus** otherwise; but, true or false, they were incidental and had not yet brought to light the real issue. For Jesus was really on trial because of his Messianic claims and activity, and his Messiahship was the real issue. So neither before the Sanhedrin nor later before Pilate did he say any word except when that question was directly raised. Nothing incidental is allowed to distract attention, divert the investigation, or obscure the issue. The Messiah, as the Messiah, is on trial, and on that issue alone he must be acquitted or condemned; there must be no uncertainty, no middle ground. And the challenge of the high priest, "Answerest thou nothing?" but serves to emphasize this situation.

The high priest too knew that this was the issue. He would have preferred to have it less clear-cut; but the

194

breakdown of his witnesses and Jesus' re-
**The High
Priest's
Question** fusal to be diverted into any incidental de-
fense forced him to come into the open. And
so now, directly and solemnly, he asked the
prisoner the central question: "Art thou the Christ, the
Son of the Blessed?"

If there had been any doubt as to his claims, if there
was later any uncertainty or evasion as to the grounds of
his condemnation, all these are removed by
**Jesus'
Answer** Jesus' answer. For now his hour was come
and he must speak in fidelity to his mission
and for the sake of his cause and his own. "I am," he
says, "and ye shall see my exaltation and my return with
power." He assumes his death—that is already settled;
but beyond his death, as in every other instance in which
he speaks of it, he sees his vindication and his triumph.

If that "I am," which "reverberates through the whole
New Testament," sealed the human fate of Jesus, it also
fixed his status; and the words that follow confirmed and
defined what the "I am" was meant to contain, and provided a deep foundation for the rebuilding of Messianic
hopes that were shattered by his death. But if these words
were the ground of encouragement and eager hope for
his followers, they were no less full of warning for his enemies. And some of the Sanhedrin, at least, would remember the context from which his words were derived.
For had not the Psalmist said, "Sit thou on my right hand
till I make thine enemies the footstool of thy feet"?
And had not Daniel seen "one like unto a son of man,
coming with the clouds of heaven, to whom was given
dominion, and glory, and a kingdom, that all the peoples

13* 195

should serve him, . . . and his kingdom that which shall not be destroyed"?

But to the high priest Jesus' words were at once welcome and intolerable, for their very blasphemy as-

"Blasphemy"

sured his condemnation, and their public and, as it would seem to him, defiant utterance left no need for further witnesses. He assumed, of course, that the words were untrue. "The attitude of Jesus to the Law and the Temple and the cherished religious traditions of Judaism left no doubt in the minds of his judges that he was a dangerous person, in whom it would be superfluous to look for any Messianic criteria."[2] And yet Jesus was now openly claiming for himself station and function even higher than that commonly assigned to the Messiah, and herein lay his "blasphemy." With his assertion of Messiahship—for the mere claim to Messiahship was not *per se* blasphemous—Jesus was claiming prerogatives of authority and of judgment that they held belonged to God alone. The earlier charge in Capernaum, in connection with the forgiveness of sins— "Who can forgive sins but one, even God?"—thus reappears in another guise. Not simply as some sort of Messiah, but as "*The Messiah, the Son of the Blessed*," with the dignity and destiny consonant with that high relationship, Jesus is condemned for blasphemy.

For when the high priest heard Jesus' words, he seized his own tunic at the throat and rent it downwards—the

"Worthy of Death"

customary and official expression of his priestly horror of blasphemy—and asked the members of the Sanhedrin what was their verdict in so plain a case; for now they all "heard the blas-

---

[2]Hastings, "Dictionary of Christ and the Gospels," II, 753.

phemy." "And they all condemned him to be worthy of death," which was as far as they could go, since they could not order his stoning in accordance with the penalty provided in the Law (Num. 15: 30; Lev. 24: 16), and, with derision and insult, turned him over to the attendants, who "received him with blows," to guard him until the approaching morning should bring opportunity to present him to the Roman governor and through him secure the confirmation and execution of their judgment.

Some incidents, at least, in these scenes are derived from the reminiscences of Peter. He had fled, with all the rest, at the arrest of Jesus; but he had turned back **Peter's Denial** and followed the arresting party into the court of the high priest's house. As he sat there beside the fire, one of the serving maids charged him with having been in the company of Jesus. But he denied it; and, torn between fear and love, withdrew into the outer court. There the maid, who seems to have been particularly zealous against "the Nazarene" and his friends, found Peter again, and called the attention of the bystanders to him. "This," she said, "is one of them," evidently reasoning that the movement against Jesus ought also include his followers: legitimate reasoning enough, and fraught with what momentous consequences! But Peter had not followed Jesus in any such heroic mind; and again he denied the accusation. But his denial was not convincing. Rather, his Galilean brogue lent color to the girl's charge. Jesus was from Galilee and had a wide following in that section, as the events of the last few days were sufficient to show even without any knowledge of his previous career. This stranger was evidently a Galilean; his speech proved that. Hence they concluded that the girl was right, and said to Peter, "You certainly are one of them; for you are a Galilean." But Peter met the increasing menace of the situation with increasing emphasis of denial, and now swore that he did not even know the man of whom they spoke. "And straightway the second time the cock crew"; and the sound brought to Peter's troubled mind his Master's prophecy; "and when he thought thereon, he wept."

Peter's denial was not merely the exposure of the groundlessness of his earlier boasting; his flight had been enough for that. It was also, and especially, a demonstration of the foreknowledge of Jesus by the exact fulfillment of his prophecy.

Jesus'
Prophecy
Fulfilled

Others might even then be deriding his prophetic powers (14: 65); but Peter's experience shows the vanity of their derision. He had denied his Master's forecast, and yet it had come to pass. The word of the Lord was sure. Thus Peter's denial, as a fulfillment of prophecy, is set over against the foolish derision of Jesus' enemies and supports the expectation that the Master's other prophetic utterances (14: 62) will also be fulfilled.

Early in the morning the Sanhedrin had Jesus bound and presented him before Pontius Pilate, the Roman procurator.[3] They must, of course, prefer charges with the delivery of their prisoner,

Jesus
Before
Pilate

and the sort of charge that would best insure his condemnation had been matter of their deliberation. No merely religious charge would be suf-

---

[3]The procurator's official seat was at Cæsarea. His presence in Jerusalem at this passover time was, significantly, due to fear of a popular disturbance, which might take the form of a Messianic insurrection, among the throngs that filled the city.

ficient. Pilate would have treated such accusations as Gallio later did in the case of Paul (Acts 18: 12–17). Some evil act must be alleged, or, better still, some political aspect must be given the case to enlist the procurator's interest and insure the condemnation of the prisoner.

But, as has been indicated, Jesus' Messianic claims and activity provided the most natural and the most dangerous material for just such political **Political Aspects** accusation. Religiously, the Sanhedrin might call such claims "blasphemy"—that would have little or no meaning for Pilate; but politically such claims might be represented as seditious, and that was a point at which Roman authority was always most sensitive and most severe. And, indeed, common Jewish Messianism was seditious from the Roman standpoint; for its aim was the overthrow of Roman domination and the reëstablishment of a kingdom of and for the Jews under the Messiah as the king. And under various leaders, and in sporadic and irregular forms, such political Messianism found frequent violent expression during the two centuries from the fall of the Maccabees (63 B.C.) to the revolt of Bar-Cochba (135 A.D.); and was always met with inexorable severity. The blood of those Galileans that Pilate had mingled with their sacrifices (Luke 13: 1) may be an illustration. And now Jesus certainly claimed to be the Messiah: that his accusers would have no difficulty in proving.

This then was the central charge that they laid before Pilate: Jesus was the Messiah, in the common sense, "the King of the Jews." The "many things" of **The Accusation** which they accused him were probably either specifications under this main charge or wee

199

designed to exhibit him as a dangerous and generally un-
desirable person who ought to be removed. But they
were incidental; and consequently, as before the Sanhedrin,
they are all ignored, and the main charge is again set in
proper perspective by the fact that it is the only point to
which Jesus speaks in all this accusation.

Pilate could not be expected to discriminate among
the various types of Messianism; but the idea that the
Messianic claims of Jesus, if proved as charged,
involved any menace to Roman supremacy
seemed to him absurd. "YOU," he asks,
"are the King of the Jews?" The emphasis is upon the
"You," and something in the appearance or situation of
Jesus prompted the form of the question.

Pilate's Question

And Jesus answered, "You are right"; as if he said,
"You have correctly stated the real accusation against
me." He could not, without qualification,
assent to the title as Pilate would naturally
understand it and as the charge was meant
by his accusers to be understood, and yet he could not
deny the title as he himself would interpret it. An effort
to explain had little chance of understanding or acceptance.
He could only say, "That is the accusation," and leave
the judgment with the governor.

Jesus' Answer

And so neither to this central charge—to which, in a
sense, he must plead guilty—nor to the subsidiary charges
did he offer any defense. But Pilate, marveling at the prisoner's silence, drew from the
situation two very significant conclusions.
The first has already been indicated: Jesus' "kingship
of the Jews" involved no political threat to the Roman
power. And the second was no less significant: All these

Pilate's Conclusion

200

charges against Jesus were but the expression of the "envy" of his accusers and should be estimated accordingly. After all, it was only a Jewish quarrel—the leaders in authority trying to use him to do away with another leader whose growing popularity threatened their position; and in this quarrel "the King of the Jews" was a mere "question about words and names" (compare Acts 18: 14–16) and therefore he need pass no judgment on it.

Pilate's sympathies were undoubtedly with Jesus, probably more from dislike and distrust of his accusers than from any appreciative regard for his **Withholds Judgment** prisoner. And it is to be observed that he did not formally condemn Jesus, or yield to the demand for his execution merely upon the insistence of his official accusers. He was unwilling to be used as a tool for the mere accomplishment of their envious purposes. On the contrary, he made a definite effort to free Jesus, or else to bring the accusation into such form that he must condemn him under the law (compare, "Why, what evil hath he done?"). And as he saw no such necessity in the evidently malicious railing of Jesus' accusers, it seemed likely that he would dismiss the case and that the Sanhedrin would thus lose their prey.

Before Pilate rendered his decision a new factor was introduced into the case. It was the procurator's custom **A New Factor** at passover time to release a prisoner at the request of the people, and they had the privilege of naming the prisoner whom he should release. While the case of Jesus was still before him, a company of petitioners came up to his judgment seat to request the release of the prisoner for that year. They seem to have named no prisoner in their first request,

201

and were probably not aware of the arrest of Jesus. But their appearance was opportune, and their request gave Pilate a chance to release Jesus and thus, with popular support, escape a situation that he did not like and defeat the envious machinations of the high priests. And so he asked them, "Will ye that I release unto you the King of the Jews?" And the fate of Jesus hung upon their answer, for Pilate would have been glad to release him at their request.

But the chief priests saw the danger to their case, and they promptly put another name upon the lips of the petitioners and urged them to request "that he should rather release Barabbas unto them."

Jesus, or Barabbas

This Barabbas had been involved in "the insurrection" (the definite article is used, indicating that the readers of the account would know of the disturbance, and hence, perhaps, no details are here given), had been arrested, and was now in prison along with the other insurrectionists. In the disturbance murder had been committed, and it may be that Barabbas and (at least) two others of the band had been condemned to death and were now awaiting execution by crucifixion. But he seems to have been of the "popular hero" type (Professor Bacon compares him to Robin Hood); and the people readily listened to the suggestion of the chief priests and pressed for his release.

But that would leave the case of Jesus still undecided. "What, then," says Pilate, "shall I do unto him whom ye call the King of the Jews? If I release Barabbas, what shall I do with Jesus?"

"Crucify Him"

"Crucify him," cried the crowd in answer, meaning "Execute him," since crucifixion was the Roman mode of executing provincial criminals. Release Barabbas, and inflict his penalty on Jesus.

"Why, what evil hath he done?" is Pilate's last challenge, not to the chief priests but to the crowd. If Jesus had done anything wrong, they certainly ought to be able to show it to justify this demand for his execution. But their petition has now become the cry of the pack. They want Barabbas—let Jesus take his place. "Crucify him, crucify him," they cry exceedingly.

And Pilate, seeing that his very effort to release Jesus is about to precipitate the tumult that his presence in Jerusalem was designed to restrain, yielded **Pilate Yields** to the clamor of the crowd what he had not granted to the accusation of the chief priests, and, "wishing to content the multitude, released unto them Barabbas, and delivered Jesus, when he had scourged him, to be crucified." And so, by indirection, the chief priests attained their end. Jesus is to be executed, not for any wrongdoing, but solely as "the King of the Jews"; and not because that title was understood by the governor as involving anything that should bring down upon him the just penalty of Roman law, but because the governor, though protesting, thought it easier and better to yield to the pressure that was brought to bear upon him. So far as the Roman law was concerned, Jesus was not condemned for sedition: he was crucified to satisfy and quiet a turbulent Jewish crowd, who were, in turn, instruments of their leaders' malice.

And Pilate's decision was final. The power of life and **The Mockery** death over provincials within his jurisdiction was in his hands. And so Jesus was forthwith delivered to the Roman soldiers who were to carry out the governor's sentence. And they, after they had made cruel and contemptuous sport of him as "King of the Jews," took him and the two robbers (perhaps of those insurrectionists with whom Barabbas was associated) who were to die with him, and led them forth to execution.

The place of crucifixion was called Golgotha, or Skull, and was located beside a highroad outside the walls of the city. There preparation for the execution had been made by the planting in the ground of the upright beams of the three crosses that would be required, though, if Golgotha was a regular place of execution, these beams may have been there as permanent fixtures. It was the task of the condemned to carry the transverse beam of his own cross to the place of his execution, and thus burdened Jesus and the two robbers set out for their death. But Jesus, because of exhaustion, had to be relieved of this burden. And for this purpose the guards impressed a certain Simon of Cyrene, whom they met on the way and who is identified as the father of the evidently well-known Alexander and Rufus, and compelled him to carry the cross for Jesus.

When they reached Golgotha, Jesus was offered the customary sedative drink that the women of Jerusalem provided for those about to be executed; but he refused it, choosing rather to meet his death in full possession of his faculties. Then the four soldiers to whom his execution was committed stripped him of his clothing, took the crossbeam from Simon's shoulders, laid Jesus upon it, and nailed his stretched-out hands to either end. Lifting the transverse

Via Dolorosa

An Eyewitness

The Crucifixion

beam, they attached it to the upright, seated Jesus upon the saddle peg fixed therein to relieve the strain upon the hands and arms, and tied or nailed his feet to the upright beam. On this beam, above Jesus' head, they nailed the board that set forth the "crime" for which he was crucified, and it bore the words, "The King of the Jews." The two robbers were crucified with him, one on either side.

This part of their task finished, the soldiers, who must still keep watch lest friends attempt a rescue, turn to the

Mockery distribution of their gruesome perquisites, the garments of the crucified, and decide by lot what each shall take. And the crowd—those who passed along the road, the instigators of the crucifixion, and even the robbers who were crucified with him— mocked the helplessness of Jesus. If he had any power, surely he would use it now for his own deliverance. "He saved others; himself he cannot save" is an incredible paradox to the selfish-minded; but it lights the cross with an inextinguishable glory!

The crucifixion had taken place at 9 o'clock in the morning: and for six hours Jesus hung suffering and

"He Calleth Elijah" silent, the last three hours in a strange miraculous darkness that covered all the land.

At 3 o'clock in the afternoon the watching soldiers and the bystanders heard what they thought was his cry for help: "Eloi, Eloi, lama sabachthani." And when some said, "He is calling Elijah," one of the soldiers quickly dipped a sponge into the jar of sour wine that they had at hand for their refreshment, and, putting it upon a short stem of hyssop (for the crucified was lifted only a foot or two above the ground), pressed it to Jesus' lips, saying to his companions, "Let us see whether Elijah will come to his rescue." But no Elijah came.

But what Jesus said was more profoundly tragic than any fruitless call for Elijah. His cry, "My God, my God, why hast thou forsaken me?" was in keeping **"My God, My God, Why Hast Thou Forsaken Me?"** with the agony in Gethsemane. It is the intense resurgence of that perplexity and distress. But his words do not indicate the triumph of despair. They rather reflect his resistance to its last dreadful assault. "When Jesus uses as his prayer the words of the twenty-second Psalm, he is quoting from the hymn book of his people a song which prompts the despairing soul to recover its trust in God, as every other prayer does at a time of great distress. It is in order to help him cling to this trust in God that Jesus now appropriates the words of another."[4] And just as the psalmist was not overwhelmed, but came up out of his darkness into the quiet and peaceful sunlight of **Dead** divine favor, so we should assume that Jesus went through both stages of his experience. But Mark adds only, "And Jesus uttered a loud voice, and gave up the ghost."

"And the veil of the temple was rent in two —signifying the removal of that barrier between man and God and the opening of a new and better way. **"This Man Was a Son of God"** And the centurion who had charge of the execution, when he saw that Jesus had died so soon, with a loud shout, and as the darkness gave place to light, said, "Truly this man was a son of God." In this intensely dramatic climax of the story of Jesus'

O. Holtzmann, "Life of Jesus," p. 489.

earthly life, we have the echo and the confirmation of the story's opening. "The beginning of the gospel of Jesus Christ, the Son of God. . . . Truly this man was a son of God." Mark has proved his thesis. Jesus *was* the Christ, the Son of God, living and dying; and the Roman officer's testimony, though his words lacked the fullness of Christian content, was the first note of what should become a mighty chorus among the Gentiles, acclaiming the Crucified, despite his crucifixion, nay, rather because of it, the *Son of the living God*.

"And he began to teach them, that the Son of man must suffer many things, and be rejected by the elders, and the chief priests, and the scribes, and be killed, and after three days rise again" (8, 31). The first part of this forecast has now been realized; it remains to record the resurrection.

"And Rise Again"

The men disciples of Jesus had all left him and fled; but a number of women disciples—among them Mary Magdalene, Mary the mother of James the less and Joses, and Salome—who had come up from Galilee to Jerusalem with him, followed him to Golgotha and witnessed his crucifixion from a distance. Thus they saw him taken down from the cross and laid in a tomb near by.

The Watching Women

The Burial

Jesus had expired at 3 o'clock on Friday afternoon, and the Sabbath began at 6 o'clock. If, therefore, his body was not to be left hanging on the cross over the Sabbath, which, from the standpoint of Jewish law, would have been a defilement of the land (Deut. 21: 23), and, from the standpoint of regard for Jesus, would have been a grievous wound to every tender feeling, some one must come forward at once who could secure permission to

207

take down the body and give it decent, if hasty, burial. The watching women themselves were in no position to do this. But there was a certain reputable member of the Sanhedrin, Joseph of Arimathæa, who had perhaps been absent from the trial of Jesus, but whose attitude toward him is indicated in the statement that "he also himself was looking for the kingdom of God," who had both the standing and the desire to perform the last sad rites for the great Proclaimer of the Kingdom. He therefore went to Pilate and requested that the corpse of Jesus be turned over to him.

Pilate was surprised at so early a request, for the crucified usually lived for many hours, sometimes for days, and probably regarded it as a scheme of the friends of Jesus for his rescue. To make sure that Jesus was really dead, Pilate called in the centurion who had directed the execution and asked for his official report. And when he had learned from the centurion that Jesus had already been dead some time, for "even was now come," he ordered the corpse to be delivered to Joseph. And Joseph thereupon bought a new linen cloth and, returning to Golgotha, took down the body of Jesus from the cross, wrapped it in the cloth, and laid it in a near-by tomb hewn in the rock. Then, for the protection of the corpse, he rolled the great circular stone that served as a door over the mouth of the tomb and departed from the scene. And the watching women "beheld where he was laid."

During the Sabbath they rested, and perhaps considered what more they might do for the Master they loved. They knew where he had been laid, and love would prompt them to visit his resting place. But they did not know what attention his body

"He Is Risen"

208

had received; and the necessary haste of its entombment would suggest that it might be their sad privilege to give it more becoming preparation for its last long sleep. That was all that they could do, and their love would do no less.

And so very early on Sunday morning they bought the spices that they thought they would need for the anointing of the body, and made their way toward the tomb. As they drew near, they wondered how they could get inside the tomb to the body of Jesus, for the stone they had seen rolled before the door was too great for their strength. "Who shall roll us away the stone?" they said among themselves. But when they looked up, they saw that the stone was already rolled away, and the entrance to the tomb was open. And when, love overcoming their anxious surprise, they entered the tomb, they saw a young man sitting on the right side, clothed in the raiment that heavenly visitors wear; and they were dumb with amazement.

But the young man reminded them of their purpose: "Ye seek Jesus, the Nazarene, who hath been crucified." But such search is vain in this depository for the dead, for "he is risen; he is not here." And that they might be the more fully assured, he invited them to see "the place where they laid him."

But the faith of the Church in a Risen Lord was not to rest solely upon the testimony of the women concerning an empty tomb. For the young man intrusted them with a message to Jesus' disciples "and Peter"—the fugitive, the denier, the heartbroken: "Go, tell his disciples and Peter, he goeth before you into Galilee: *there shall ye* [the

209

recipients of the message] *see him, as he said unto you*" (see Mark 14: 28).

"And they [the women] went out, and fled from the tomb; for trembling and astonishment had come upon them: and they said nothing to any one; for they were afraid."

And thus abruptly the Gospel of Mark comes to an end, mutilated, we know not how, in the very earliest stages of its history. At later dates other and unknown hands undertook to make good the loss by the addition of various endings to the Gospel. The longest ending, which appears in our King James Version, was written about the middle of the second century, and has been attributed, on insufficient grounds, to a certain Ariston (or Aristion), a presbyter of that period. It is compiled almost entirely from material supplied by the Lukan writings and the Fourth Gospel; and we, like its compiler, must turn to these and other early sources for accounts of the appearances of our risen Lord.

210